TRINIDAD & TOBAGO

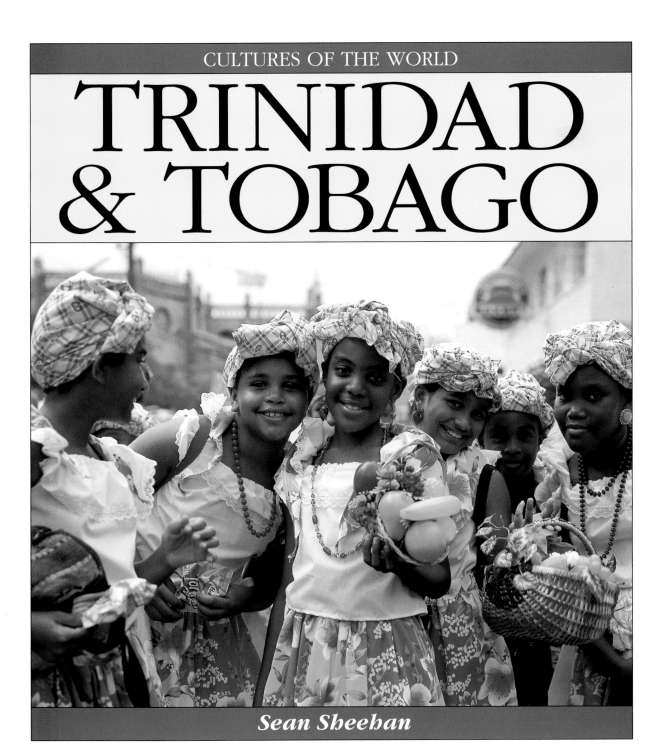

Sean Sheehan

MARSHALL CAVENDISH
New York • London • Sydney

Reference edition reprinted 2001 by
Marshall Cavendish Corporation
99 White Plains Road
Tarrytown
New York 10591

© Times Media Private Limited 2001

Originated and designed by
Times Books International, an imprint of
Times Media Private Limited, a member of the
Times Publishing Group

Printed in Malaysia

Library of Congress Cataloging-in-Publication Data:
Sheehan, Sean, 1951–
    Trinidad & Tobago / Sean Sheehan.
       p. cm. — (Cultures of the world)
    Includes bibliographical references and index.
    ISBN 0-7614-1194-1
    1. Trinidad & Tobago—Juvenile literature. [1. Trinidad &
Tobago.] I. Title: Trinidad & Tobago. II. Title. III. Series.

    F2119.S54 2001
    972.983—dc21
                            00-047457
                            CIP
                            AC

INTRODUCTION

THE ISLANDS OF TRINIDAD AND TOBAGO are the most southern of the Caribbean islands, lying only a few miles off the coast of South America, near Venezuela. They have been attracting settlers for well over two millennia, and this has led to a lively and varied population from many corners of the globe. Europeans, Africans, Indians, and Chinese have all made their homes here, and a racial and cultural melting pot is the result. Unlike other parts of the world, the blending of cultures has not produced conflict, and the people celebrate their sense of togetherness and national identity with much gusto and warmth.

Distinct from other Caribbean islands, Trinidad and Tobago has managed to welcome overseas visitors without selling its soul to tourism and diluting its own cultural identity in the process. The people of Trinidad and Tobago know how to enjoy life and are blessed with a hospitable environment that helps to make this possible.

CONTENTS

A young girl with her hair done up prettily.

CONTENTS

Stilt-walkers gracing the annual Carnival in Port-of-Spain.

GEOGRAPHY

TRINIDAD AND TOBAGO ARE TWO RELATIVELY SMALL ISLANDS off the north coast of Venezuela in the Caribbean Sea. They are the two southernmost islands of a chain of islands known as the Windward Islands, a chain that includes the islands of Grenada, Dominica and St. Lucia, and others. These in turn are part of a 2,000-mile (3,218 km) long chain of islands known as the West Indies, which includes Cuba and Jamaica and stretches from southeast of Florida to the northern coast of Venezuela. The West Indies separate the Caribbean Sea from the Atlantic Ocean.

Trinidad is separated from Venezuela by the Gulf of Paria, which extends 100 miles (161 km) east-west and 40 miles (64 km) north-south. The island has a total area of 1,864 square miles (4,828 square km) and is the more industrialized of the two islands. Tobago, lying 7 miles (11 km) northeast of Trinidad, is smaller, only 116 square miles (300 square km).

Left: **Caroni Swamp is one of the many places in Trinidad where the natural environment is still unspoiled.**

Opposite: **Crystal clear waters crashing against the rocky shores of Tobago.**

TERRAIN

The islands of Trinidad and Tobago are basically extensions of mainland South America. Trinidad has three ranges of hills running across it from west to east; the most significant is the Northern Range, part of a range that starts in the Andes Mountains and extends along the Paria Peninsula to the islands. The Northern Range has an average height of about 1,500 feet (457 m), and its highest point is El Cerro del Aripo (Mount Aripo) at 3,084 feet (940 m). The second range of hills, known as the Central Range, has its highest point, Mount Tamana (1,009 feet/307 m), at the eastern end. The Southern Range follows the southern coast of the island and is largely a series of low hills. Those on the east are known as the Trinity Hills. The low-lying land between the ranges tends to be swampy, fed by the many rivers that run off from the hills. Northwest of the island is the large Caroni Swamp, and in the east of the island the Nariva Swamp.

PITCH LAKES

Three pitch lakes exist in the world. One is in California, another in Venezuela, and the third in Trinidad. Unlike the other two, the pitch lake in Trinidad is still active. Pitch lakes occur when oil oozes up to the surface of the ground and the more volatile elements evaporate, leaving a residue of naturally occurring asphalt. Trinidad's Pitch Lake covers 116 acres (47 hectares) and is thought to contain 6,700,000 tons of asphalt, which is replenished continuously. It is possible to walk across the lake. When Sir Walter Raleigh visited Trinidad in the 16th century, he used the asphalt he found in the lake to caulk his boats and declared it the best he had ever seen.

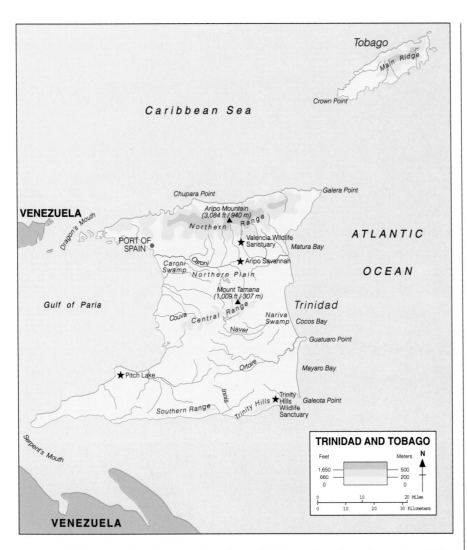

In addition to the hundreds of small rivers flowing down its hills, Trinidad has only two major rivers. The Ortoire in the south stretches for 31 miles (50 km) and empties into the Atlantic Ocean. The second major river is the Caroni in the northwest. It rises in the Northern Range and flows 25 miles (40 km) toward the mangrove swamps along the northwestern coast.

Tobago is a further extension of the Northern Range of Trinidad. It has a central ridge that runs southwest to northeast; it is called the Main Ridge.

HABITATS

Trinidad and Tobago has an abundant plant and animal life mainly because of the undeveloped nature of the islands and the variety of habitats. Unlike the other islands in the West Indies that are volcanic in origin, these islands form part of the lower slopes of the Andes Mountains. Four ranges of hills, two large rivers and hundreds of small rivers, an extensive coastline, mangrove swamps, and coral reefs provide an abundance of habitats for wild creatures.

RAINFOREST

The four ranges of hills are densely covered with rainforests. The tallest trees form a canopy over the forest that reaches as high as 150 feet (46 m). Orchids and bromeliads grow in the trees, fastened to the branches and

The conspicuous nests of the oriole hanging from a tree.

SAVANNAH

Typical savannah vegetation is found in the Aripo Savannah, a nature reserve east of Port-of-Spain. Monice palms grow at the edges of the high grassland, and sundew flourishes in this inhospitable land because it is able to trap insects to provide nourishment. There are many bird species here—hummingbirds, the Savannah hawk, red bellied macaws, and parrots.

taking their nourishment from the air and dying leaves. Lianas wind their way up tree trunks from the ground. The trees of the rainforest tend to flower in the spring, although in the dry season from December to March, an introduced species, the immortelle tree (*erythrina micropteryx*), covers the forest in orange flowers. In March another tree bursts into bloom—the poui tree, with striking yellow blossoms. Before it flowers, it loses its leaves, making the blossoms all the more striking.

An amazing variety of birds live in the forest, mostly high up in the canopy where they feed on the fruit of the trees as it comes into season. In the hills, at least 2,000 feet (609 m) above sea level, there are yellow-legged thrush, nightingale thrush, and blue tanagers. At lower levels but less easy to spot is the unusual oilbird (*steatornis caripensis*), which lives deep in caves and forages for fruit at night. Young oilbirds were once used for both meat and fuel oil, but they are rare now. A large oilbird has a wingspan of 3 feet (1 m). The bird of paradise on Tobago is an introduced species.

The rainforest is also home to a variety of animals. Ocelot that live in the forest often make their way to cultivated land where this protected species is shot by farmers to protect their domestic animals.

A proud hunter with his catch, an agouti.

SWAMPLAND

Both Trinidad and Tobago have areas of swampland where rivers meander toward the sea, creating large wet areas that are home to many species of plants and animals. The most characteristic plantlife in these areas is the mangrove tree. The tree is able to survive in salt marshes because its roots grow from the trunk above the water line and take in air from the atmosphere. The tree produces seeds that germinate while still attached to the trunk, sending roots into the mud before the seedling falls away from the tree. This prevents the seed from being washed out to sea when the high tide sweeps into the swamp.

The Caroni Swamp in northwestern Trinidad is a nature reserve consisting of 12,000 acres (4,860 hectares) of lagoon, forest, and marshland. Scarlet Ibis, the national bird of Trinidad and Tobago, lives here in flocks. Among the other 140 bird species to be found at Caroni are the cormorant, anhinga, and boat-billed heron. In the waters of the swamp are edible fish and other marine life, including huge garrupas, snapper, tree oysters, mussels, and blue crab. Caiman, a type of crocodile, also live in the swamp. Iguanas and manatees can also be found.

Banana trees, with their distinctive hanging flower, commonly grow along the shoreline.

THE COASTLINE

Tobago has extensive coral reef that are home to some very colorful fish; many are favorites in aquariums all over the world. Grunts, triggerfish, parrot fish, and butterfly fish are all quite common. Buccoo, situated in southwestern Tobago, is now a protected area, although tourism in past years caused much damage to fire and staghorn coral, sea fans, and sea whips on the reef as well as many other species in the deeper waters.

Five species of turtle nest on the beaches of the islands. The largest is the leatherback, which can grow to seven feet and weigh 1,200 pounds (545 kg). Other species are the green turtle, loggerhead turtle, hawksbill turtle, and olive ridley, the smallest of the five. All of them share a common nesting habit of coming ashore to bury their eggs in the sand. Turtles are protected during the nesting season but are hunted at other times of the year.

On the shoreline, there are several very distinctive trees to be found. Almond and mango trees line the shores. This type of almond tree does not produce edible fruit. Coconut palms are also common, as are royal palms and traveler's palms.

CLIMATE

Trinidad and Tobago has a tropical climate of high relative humidity and distinct seasons, with a dry season between December and May and a wet season between June and November. During the wet season, it rains for a short time in the late afternoon each day. June is the wettest month, while February is the driest. During the dry season, temperatures tend to fall a little to an average of 68°F (20°C). April is the hottest month with temperature highs of around 85°F (29°C).

The prevailing winds on the islands are northeast trade winds with a velocity of about 10 to 20 miles (16 to 22 km) per hour. They lower the temperature and bring rain to the eastern side of the islands.

Trinidad and Tobago is usually outside the hurricane zone. Hurricanes tend to form between June and September either to the north of the islands or in the eastern Atlantic Ocean near the Cape Verde islands, but occasionally the country is hit by a hurricane, notably in 1847, 1867, and 1963 when Hurricane Flora killed 7,000 people in the Caribbean.

URBAN CENTERS

The major urban center and capital of Trinidad and Tobago is Port-of-Spain, located on the west coast of Trinidad at the bottom of the peninsula that extends to the Dragon's Mouth passage in the Gulf of Paria. Port-of-Spain is also the chief port of the islands. The city lies on a coastal plain with hills to the east, which form the suburbs of the city. The old part of the city is now the business area and also houses government buildings. There are many well laid out parks, including a botanic garden. The largest airport in the Caribbean is 16 miles (26 km) outside the city at Piarco. Port-of-Spain's estimated population is 51,076.

At the other end of the Gulf of Paria is Trinidad's second city, San Fernando. Like Port-of-Spain, it is an important shipping center and is located on a flat plain with the hills of the Central Range to the east. San Fernando is an administrative center for the south of the island and was once the home of a community of Carib Indians. The city services the extensive oilfields of the south of the island. Its population is 33,000.

15

Trinidad's third largest and most newly developed town is Chaguanas, located halfway between San Fernando and Port-of-Spain. It is now an important business center servicing the oil industry, and like San Fernando and Arima, Chaguanas was once home to a group of Carib Indians. Arima, previously the third most important city in Trinidad, is now less vibrant, although it is still an important stop on the island's highway system.

The southern end of Trinidad is dominated by heavy industry, with several towns supporting the workers. Point Lisas is the major industrial centre. Another urban center is Point-à-Pierre.

The main town in Tobago is Scarborough, which has a deep water harbor on the Atlantic coast. The town sits on the steep sides of a hill overlooking Scarborough Harbor. It became the capital of the island in 1796, replacing Mount St. George farther to the northeast. Scarborough has a population of 17,000 and is more rural than the towns of Trinidad. Most

Arima, a town on Trinidad.

BIRD OF PARADISE ISLAND

This island, sometimes known as Little Tobago, is situated about one mile (1.6 km) off the northeast coast of Tobago, near a tiny village called Speyside. The island has been designated a wildlife sanctuary and is home to an introduced species of greater birds of paradise brought to the island in 1909 and much harmed by Hurricane Flora in 1963. The island is uninhabited by humans but 58 species of birds live there.

buildings, other than government ones or the few modern ones, are simple one-story structures with tin roofs. To the west of Scarborough is the international airport. The area around it has many tourist-oriented beach resorts and hotels with close access to the reefs at Buccoo.

Farther northeast along the coast is Roxborough, the second largest settlement in Tobago. On the northern peninsula is Charlotteville. Charlotteville is slightly bigger than a village and is isolated by the surrounding mountains. The chief occupation here is fishing.

HISTORY

TRINIDAD IS PROBABLY THE FIRST ISLAND IN THE CARIBBEAN to have been occupied by humans. Prior to 300 B.C., hunter-gatherer Meso-Indians lived on the island of Trinidad, leaving behind them stone tools and shell middens.

A second wave of settlers arrived on Tobago, from South America around 300 B.C. These people were farmers who could make pots and cloth and who cultivated potatoes and cassava, which they used to make bread. They colonized most of the lesser Antilles and spoke dialects of the Arawak language. However, around A.D. 1000, another group who spoke Carib dialects moved onto the islands.

The islands continued to be developed by these two groups of people for 500 years. It was their descendants that Christopher Columbus met when he arrived on the island of Trinidad in 1498.

Left: **The Carib were one of the first few pioneers to occupy Trinidad.**

Opposite: **An illustration depicting a gathering of West Indian slaves at an early evangelistic meeting.**

SPANISH COLONIALISM

The settlements that Columbus encountered were impermanent as people constantly moved to new areas of cultivation when the old areas became infertile. They lived in small village communities. Work was divided, with women doing domestic chores and the farming, while men hunted.

The Spanish did not settle in Trinidad for a century or so, though they raided it often for slaves. The first Spanish settlement was established in 1592 at St. Joseph on Trinidad. For two centuries the Spanish colony survived, but with little investment, and the town was regularly attacked by the British and Dutch. Missionaries arrived and established missions around the island. One was attacked by the Indians it sought to convert in 1699. Its missionaries, the governor, and several soldiers were killed.

Gradually settlers arrived and set up tobacco plantations, but these failed. Cocoa plantations were started later and were more successful until 1725, when the entire industry was wiped out by a crop disease. This was followed by smallpox in 1739, which killed many of the planters.

A FRENCH AND BRITISH COLONY

By 1777 Port-of-Spain was established as a small fort, with a church and about 80 thatched houses. With the other Caribbean islands having more to offer to settlers, it proved difficult to attract Spanish people to Trinidad, so the governor began to encourage French settlers who were Catholics. Any white immigrant was offered 130 acres (53 hectares) for each family member who came, and 650 acres (263 hectares) for each slave they brought.

Trinidad became more French than Spanish as settlers from the other West Indian islands arrived. The French language was used, and the French tradition of Carnival was introduced. People of color or mixed ancestry were also attracted to the island by its lack of discrimination.

In 1790 slave trading was allowed on the island. Prior to this, slaves were brought in by their masters but never bought and sold here. Cotton and sugar plantations began to thrive as slavery made cultivation possible.

Around this time Britain and France were at war, and the fighting often involved Trinidad, technically still a Spanish colony. In 1797 Trinidad was invaded by the British, and the Spanish surrendered. The Spanish were offered friendly terms of surrender, but the governor left in charge of the island treated the residents cruelly, particularly anyone he feared might be planning rebellion. Many people of color were imprisoned and tortured. This cruel rule lasted six years until the governor was replaced. In the same year, 1803, Tobago was taken by the British. Trinidad subsequently became a Crown Colony, ruled directly by Britain and administered by a governor.

In the 1700s pirates were the bane of traders and immigrants.

THE SLAVE TRADE

Trinidad's development had been hindered by the restrictions on slave trading, which had lasted till 1790. By the time of British rule, abolitionists had begun to lobby the British government to restrict the slave trade in Trinidad. Other West Indian islands had already developed slave economies, and the abolitionists wished to stop another slave economy from developing in Trinidad. The other West Indian colonies agreed, for if Trinidad could not develop its sugar and cotton industries, there would be less competition for them. In 1806 the slave trade was forbidden to Trinidad and Tobago, although slaves already on the island were not freed. In 1812 the British issued an order that all slaves in Trinidad should be registered, and no more slaves could be made use of on the island beyond those registered. The order was ignored; illegal slave trading continued.

In the 1700s most slaves were working in sugar plantations.

POST SLAVERY

The repercussions of the injustice of slavery continued in Trinidad for years after abolition. The former slaves rebelled against working for their masters, and slavery was brought to an end in 1838, two years earlier than the legislation demanded. The former slaves now found themselves in a strong bargaining position. They could negotiate for good wages because there had always been a shortage of slaves, unlike other West Indian colonies where even after freedom, former slaves still lived in poverty because there were too many of them to bargain for better wages. Some former slaves on Trinidad took up farm work on the plantations, some others moved to the cities and found work, while still others bought a smallholding or squatted on unused land. In 1869 the squatters were allowed to buy their plots of land at a cost of one pound per 5 acres (2 hectares).

Meanwhile the sugar and cotton plantations were suffering from a shortage of labor. Recruitment was attempted all over the Caribbean to attract American blacks, the Chinese on Madeira, and liberated slaves from other colonies, but those who came generally found work in the cities or bought their own smallholding. In 1848 the British government began to encourage indentured laborers. In exchange for their passage, laborers from India had to work for the landowner for a certain number of years. The arrangement continued until 1917. When their period of indenture ended, the Indians followed the example of the former slaves and also bought plots of land. Thus more indentured laborers had to be brought from India, leading to modern Trinidad's ethnic mix.

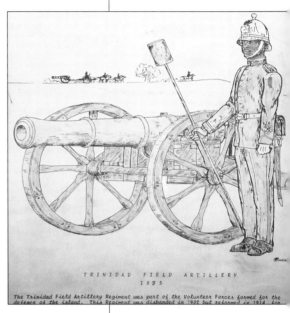

TRINIDAD FIELD ARTILLERY
1895

The Trinidad Field Artillery Regiment was part of the Volunteer Forces formed for the defence of the island. This Regiment was disbanded in 1902 but reformed in 1914 for...

The end of slavery liberated former slaves for other jobs, one of which was to join the defense forces.

TOBAGO

Tobago had a more difficult time. Up until 1803, the island changed hands many times among the French, Dutch, English, and Spanish, often suffering badly at each exchange of ruler. A slave economy emerged based on the cultivation of sugar and cotton, and although liberal legislation was passed allowing slaves to own land and providing allowances for their wellbeing, a slave rebellion was uncovered in 1801 just before it was to take place. Six rebel leaders were executed and many more were flogged and banished. Emancipation came to Tobago at the same time as to the other colonies. Because Tobago had become more of a slave economy than Trinidad, it suffered more as a result.

Loading in a modern day sugarcane plantation.

Like Trinidad, immigration was encouraged, but unlike Trinidad, the wages were so low that few people could be persuaded to come. In 1847 a hurricane destroyed many plantations, and the falling price of sugar increased Tobago's distress. For a few years a system where farm workers shared the crops with the landowner seemed to work, but eventually the landowners were making so little money that the scheme fell through. In 1889 Tobago was made a ward of Trinidad, and the two islands were legally one country for the first time.

By 1900 Port-of-Spain was a major urban center and a quarter of the population lived there. Huge numbers of disenfranchised urban poor lived beside the rich, white French and English settlers. In 1903 there was a riot in Port-of-Spain over water shortages. Eighteen people were killed, and the government building was burned down. The riots, though about water, were taken to be an indication of political unrest, and plans began to instate a representative assembly in Trinidad. In 1913 the assembly was installed with a very limited franchise.

INDENTURED WORKERS

Once slavery was abolished on the islands, Britain turned to India, a country where conditions were so poor that people were willing to leave their country to work. These Indians were largely men who were indentured for five years to a plantation owner. After that, they could choose reindenture or other work as long as they could pay a special tax. After five more years, they were allowed a free passage back to India. If the laborer broke his contract, it was a criminal offense and he would be imprisoned. Conditions were harsh, pay was low, and there were few women with whom to make marriages. Unhappiness stalked their domestic life as well. Between 1872 and 1900, 87 Indian wives of indentured workers were murdered, mostly by their husbands because of their infidelities with other indentured workers. The Indians were despised in society. Nevertheless, after the indenture was over, few returned to India as their connections were now severed. Most stayed to become farm workers or moved to the towns where they took up other trades.

ROOPER A.S.BOURNE

PTE. J.A.WADE

2nd.LIEUT. G.G.BUSHE

: J F.EVERSLEY

PTE. V. REDMAN

SERGT. MAJOR C.E.LAURENCE

AN OIL ECONOMY

The world's first oil well was sunk in 1857 at La Brea in southern Trinidad, long before the internal combustion engine would provide a sufficient incentive for the drillers. Oil burning engines became commercially viable in the 1890s, and Trinidad's economy changed forever. When the British Navy began to buy diesel-powered ships, British money and engineering skills poured into Trinidad. During the pioneering days of the oil industry, there were many accidents, but by 1929 the technology had been developed.

RACE RELATIONS

During World War I, life became very hard for working men in Trinidad, and there was a lot of political unrest and strikes. The black men who volunteered to fight for Britain were banned from killing Germans for fear that they might get used to killing white men! They were kept in segregated units, commanded by white officers. In the months following the end of the war, the West Indian troops were sent to Italy to act as domestic servants to the white troops. Several rebelled and were imprisoned. The returning soldiers told stories of racial discrimination, rapidly followed by news of antiblack demonstrations in Britain. The victory celebrations in Trinidad were boycotted, and white businessmen began to feel threatened. In 1919 black dockworkers held a strike for better pay. When they were refused, they walked away from their jobs. When nonunion labor was brought in, warehouses were smashed. Workers throughout Trinidad joined in the disturbances. British troops intervened, and leading strikers were arrested and imprisoned. Strikes were made illegal, and newspapers and radical publications were banned.

In 1925 the franchise was extended, and Indians and trade union representatives were elected to the legislature. But as the worldwide depression began to hit Trinidad, workers grew poorer, and people began to suffer from hunger. In 1934 hunger marches were organized around the island. In 1937 oil workers began a sit-down strike and were chased away by the police. Two oil wells were set on fire. When police tried to arrest the leader, a crowd attacked them, and two policemen were killed. The strikes spread to other oilfields and other industries, and it began to look like a revolution. British warships were sent to Trinidad, and the strikes fizzled out. Some concessions to the workers' demands were made, and the threat of revolution disappeared. However, the unions had grown strong and remained a threat to employers right up to World War II.

Opposite: **The Roll-of-Honor of heroes who led the West Indian troops during World War I.**

WORLD WAR II

When World War II began, part of Trinidad was leased to the United States, and huge bases were built. Warships filled the Gulf of Paria and were hunted by German U boats. Things improved for Trinidadians: there was high employment and better wages and a roaring nightlife catering the American troops. The war came to an end in May 1945. Shortly afterwards, constitutional reforms provided for universal suffrage.

The Trinidadian Memorial Park, where war heroes are commemorated.

POST-WAR POLITICS

After the war, political groups and individuals with different platforms competed for seats in the legislature. By the 1956 election, there were seven parties and 39 independents. The parties represented different social and ethnic groups; the strongest was the PNM (People's Nationalist Movement), a black and nationalist party. The next most powerful group was the PDP (People's Democratic Party). The PNM formed the government, and the process toward independence in 1962 began. Two parties predominated in the islands: the PNM, made up of black nationalists intellectuals with the support of the trade unions, who wanted to take back the oilfields that had been leased by Britain to United States; and the PDP, largely white and Indian, unionist and in favor of international capital. In the 1961 election, white and Indian homes and businesses were looted. On the verge of a serious racial war, Trinidadians and Tobagans went to the poll and gave the PNM a large majority. The following year, Trinidad and Tobago became an independent state.

INDEPENDENCE

Although the PNM campaigned against foreign capital and supported trade unions when seeking power, it changed its stance once in control, inviting foreign investment and reducing the power of the trade unions. The opposition PDP faded into the background, and the islands became virtually a one-party state. After a series of strikes for better pay, the Industrial Stabilization Act was passed in 1965, making strikes impossible.

Despite rising oil revenues, things did not improve for the black majority in Trinidad. The educational system did improve their quality of training, but there were no jobs for young blacks. With the banning of strikes and no prospect of improvement, a black power movement developed. Workers began to organize strikes in contravention of the law. In 1970 there were black power demonstrations in Port-of-Spain.

Armed police during the 1970 demonstration. A state of emergency was declared in response to the demonstration. A movement called the United Labor Front was also formed as a result of the incident.

GOVERNMENT

TRINIDAD AND TOBAGO first acquired a common government in 1889. Prior to that, Tobago was a British colony unrelated to its larger neighbor. It had a bicameral legislature, while Trinidad had a simpler, single legislative assembly. The merger of the two countries meant that the government of Tobago shifted to Trinidad, although Tobago retained separate taxes and a smaller subordinate legislature.

In 1925 the national legislature was reformed and members added. This was followed by a universal suffrage in 1945. Government rule was carried out by a party based cabinet, but authority was based in Britain.

INDEPENDENCE

Independence occurred in 1962, although the links with Britain were not completely severed. The islands became part of the British Commonwealth

Left: **The White Hall is a distinct symbol of the country's independence.**

Opposite: **The stability of the country is assured under the vigilance of the police force.**

and were to be ruled by a governor-general, not elected, but appointed by Britain. The governor had a cabinet made up of elected representatives. Beneath the cabinet was a bicameral legislature, along the lines of the American system. Both houses were elected.

In 1976 the current constitution was adopted. This removed the governor-general and instituted a nonexecutive president heading a republic. The president, currently Arthur Napoleon Raymond Robinson, is elected by an electoral college of all the country's ministers. Below the president is a cabinet chosen by and headed by the prime minister. The prime minister and cabinet are responsible to parliament.

A parliament meeting.

The legislature, or parliament, consists of two houses, one, the House of Representatives with 36 members who are directly elected. Legislation originates and passes from this house to the Senate, which is made up of 31 members appointed by the president. Sixteen of these are chosen on the advice of the prime minister, six on the recommendation of the leader of the opposition, and nine by the president. Elections to the House of Representatives are held every five years.

Tobago has its own devolved House of Assembly, set up in 1980, which can legislate on some financial matters and other local issues such as urban and rural development, education, health, and housing. It has 12 elected members. In the last elections in December 1996, there were 10 NAR members, one PNM member, and one independent party member.

POLITICAL PARTIES

For several years after independence, Trinidad and Tobago had a chaotic electoral system with individuals competing for seats in parliament. Eventually a series of political parties formed, mostly along racial lines. The first parties to form before independence were the People's National Party (PNM) and the People's Democratic Party (PDP), both formed in the 1950s. The PNM contested the elections of 1956 along with seven other parties. The PNM represented the black middle classes and stood for better education and nationalism, and strongly criticized the ruling white elite. The PNM won majorities in most elections from 1956 until 1986, and so the government of Trinidad was in the hands of a party that represented black middle-class interests.

The PDP was largely Indian in makeup and for many years formed the chief opposition party. In the 1970s the PDP merged with a radical group,

Trinidad and Tobago is divided into 11 local government areas. Eight of the divisions are rural and have a county council; the other three are municipalities—Port-of-Spain, San Fernando, and Arima. These have municipal councils.

Opposite: **The district court in Port-of-Spain.**

the Action Committee of Dedicated Citizens (ACDC) and became the Democratic Liberation Party (DLP).

In Tobago, the PNM did less well and a series of coalitions led by the politician Arthur Napoleon Raymond Robinson took control of the assembly.

In 1986 the PNM lost power in Trinidad as a coalition of very diverse parties representing big business, trade unions, rural Indians, and all Toboganians called the Alliance for National Reconstruction (ANR) took power. For the first time the country was led by a multi-ethnic party but it did not last because the measures that were necessary at the time proved too unpleasant for the electorate. After a coup, the coalition collapsed and the PNM returned to power in 1991.

DEATH ROW

In 1996 a gang of nine men murdered a family in southern Williamsville, Trinidad. Found guilty of the murder, the nine men were sentenced to death, a mandatory punishment under Trinidad and Tobago law. The men's lawyers took their case to the Privy Council in London in May 1999. But more than the lives of these nine men was resting on the Privy Council's decision. Tension was high among the Caribbean countries, many of whom also use the British Privy Council as a last court of appeal, since the sovereign rights of Trinidad and Tobago would be challenged if the Privy Council commuted the sentence. The Privy Council upheld the conviction, and the nine men were executed in June 1999, despite pleas for mercy by Bishop Desmond Tutu and other international figures. The nine men were all drug racketeers, and 80% of public opinion in Trinidad supported the death penalty. The decision of the Privy Council ensured that men on death rows all over the Caribbean would now face the death penalty. In June 1999 there were at least 100 men on death row in Trinidad alone.

The 1995 election saw the emergence of another single-race party, the United National Congress (UNC). Seats in the House of Representatives were split exactly between the two parties, the PNM and the UNC, with two ANR members supporting the UNC. For the first time in Trinidad's history there is an Indian Prime Minister, Basdeo Panday.

THE JUDICIAL SYSTEM

Trinidad and Tobago's judicial system is based on the British legal system. The highest court is the Supreme Court, consisting of a High Court and a Court of Appeal. Presently the final court of appeal for Trinidadians is the Privy Council in London, but provision is being made for a Caribbean Supreme Court, which would replace the function of the privy Council.

Below the higher courts, there is a system of magistrate courts to deal with less important matters. Trinidad and Tobago has 16 judges appointed by the president based on the advice of the legal service commission. The chief justice is also appointed by the president on the advice of the prime minister. All primary posts in the judicial system are filled at the discretion of the president and prime minister.

REGIONAL POLITICS

Trinidad and Tobago's chief area of international concern in recent years has been the matter of territorial waters in dispute with Venezuela, particularly over fishing rights and oil field rights. In 1997 a commission with members from both countries was set up to look into incidents in the Gulf of Paria, the disputed area.

Also in 1997 Trinidad applied to become a member of NAFTA (North Atlantic Free Trade Association). Trinidad and Tobago has signed a bilateral trade agreement with India and is discussing possible trade links with Cuba. It is a member of Caricom, the 15-member Caribbean

President Robinson in a meeting with Britain's Prince Charles. The president has been in office since March 19, 1997.

Community, which intends to set up a single market along the lines of the European Economic Community. The Association of Caribbean States has its headquarters at Port-of-Spain.

Trinidad is a member of the Organization of American States and has signed a treaty with the United States on cooperation over international crime. Ninety percent of Trinidadian crime is drug-related.

SOME POLITICAL FIGURES

The most important political figure and charismatic leader in Trinidad and Tobago is Eric Williams, but there are many other important people who have played a part in Trinidad and Tobago's political life. Bhadase Maharaj was the president of Maha Sabha, an orthodox Hindu association. He took an active part in politics, for a time leading the PDP. He represented the Indian equivalent of Williams but was never able to mobilize Indian Muslims to his side. He was a flamboyant character and often carried guns in public. He was succeeded as leader of the now renamed DLP in 1960 by Rudranath Capildeo, another Indian, this time from an academic background. In the 1961 election, he recommended that people arm themselves against the PNM and prepare to take over the country. The DLP lost that election, even in Tobago.

Basdeo Panday was a young lawyer in 1971 when he became interested in politics and was persuaded to lead a party called the United Liberation Front (ULF), a combination of several other small parties including the DLP. In 1995 he became Trinidad's first ethnic Indian prime minister. President A.N.R. Robinson is a Tobagonian who has taken an active part in the country's politics for many years. His party, another coalition, took power in 1986, and in July 1990 President Robinson was taken hostage by a small, radical Muslim group for six days during a coup.

The national flag has three colors, white, black, and red. Red symbolizes the temperament of the country, its vitality, warmth, and courage. Black is the color of strength and unity and the wealth of the country in its oil reserves. White represents purity and equality. The three colors also represent earth (black), water (white), and fire (red), the three basic elements of life.

ECONOMY

TRINIDAD AND TOBAGO HAS A MIXED ECONOMY with some areas of the economy owned and run by the state, while the majority are run by private enterprise. The economy relies heavily on the oil industry and is subject to the fluctuations in the price of oil, sometimes enjoying a boom and at other times experiencing a depression. Compared to other countries in the Caribbean of its size, Trinidad and Tobago's economy is sophisticated, involving mineral extraction, industry, agriculture, tourism, and services, as well as oil and gas exploitation. The currency is the Trinidad and Tobago dollar. It fluctuates at about TT$6 to the U.S. dollar.

THE OIL AND GAS INDUSTRY

Oil was discovered in Trinidad in 1857 when the world's first oil well was drilled at La Brea. In 1914 the first oil refinery was built in Trinidad

Left: **Trinidad is a producer of methanol. Five plants around the country produce about 8% of the world's methanol.**

Opposite: **Heavy traffic and bustling workers epitomize the energy of the thriving economy of Trinidad.**

39

and Tobago at Point-à-Pierre. By 1946 Trinidadian oil represented 65% of the British Empire's oil production. A second refinery has been added recently at Point Fortin. For the last 25 years oil has dominated the country's economy. In 1995 the petroleum industry contributed 28% of the Gross Domestic Product (GDP).

There are 30 operating oil and gas fields, mostly in the south of Trinidad or off the southwestern coast. Current reserves of oil are thought to be about 490 million barrels, about 10 years' supply at the current rate of production. Output has already slowed by about 25%. In 1997 further exploration began, and the government sold off six areas for exploration, retaining a 50% interest. The oil industry employs about 16,000 people.

Domestic gasoline consumption takes up a significant amount of the industry's output annually.

Natural gas is another important sector of Trinidad and Tobago's economy. Reserves are estimated at 18 trillion cubic feet and are expected to last 100 years. Amoco owns about 85% of the gas produced. The gas is turned into liquefied natural gas, and about 3.5 million barrels are produced a day.

The scale and sophistication of the car industry provides skilled employment in the job market.

HEAVY INDUSTRY

Several industries have emerged as a result of the development of the oil industry. A petrochemical industry produces by-products of oil for export and local use. Methanol is produced, and Trinidad contributes 20% of the world's supply. There are eight ammonia plants throughout the islands, including the world's largest ammonia producer, with an output of 1,900 tons per day.

Other major industries include car assembly, radio and television production, paper products and printing, cement, furniture, processed food, and clothes.

Baby lettuce nursed in a market garden.

AGRICULTURE

From being a major producer of coffee, sugar, and cocoa in the last century, Trinidad and Tobago has developed a more industrialized economy. Agriculture now accounts for about 2% of GDP and employs about one-tenth of the population. Sugar is the main crop and is grown on large estates once owned by white settlers. For a time, the estates were owned by a British company, Tate and Lyle, but in the 1970s several estates were bought up by the state industry, Caroni Limited. The estates, mostly in southern Trinidad, still show the signs of the old settlers with grand houses occupied by the management and tiny shanty houses occupied by the field workers.

The sugar is harvested and sent to mills where the plant is crushed and the sugar refined. The refined sugar is exported chiefly to the United States and the European Union. About 123,000 tons of sugar are produced in Trinidad each year. Some of the by-products are used in the making of a local rum.

Other important export crops include citrus fruits, bananas, and pineapples. Cocoa has recently suffered badly from an insect pest called hibiscus mealy bug, and so the estates have diversified into cultivating oranges and lemons. Small amounts of coffee, copra, and coconuts are farmed commercially.

The rest of the island's agriculture is dedicated to small local farms, either producing a subsistence living for their owners or providing enough of a surplus to be sold in local markets. The island produces an abundance of other crops, including rice, sweet potatoes, taro, and sweetcorn, but few of these are grown commercially.

Livestock farming is also a local business. It is estimated that the islands have about 80,000 cattle, 70,000 pigs, and 13,000 sheep, all owned by small farmers for sale in local markets. Chickens are also an important staple, and buffalo are kept mainly for transportation and for ploughing fields.

Goats grazing leisurely in a goat farm in Tobago.

SUGAR PRODUCTION

Sugar grows in hot, humid climates. It is a labor-intensive industry, requiring hand cutting. In Trinidad transportation to the refineries is often by ox-cart rather than by truck. In the factory the cane is crushed between a series of rollers and the juice extracted. As the cane is crushed, hot water is sprayed over the fibers to dissolve any remaining sugar. The leftover pulp of the plant is called bagasse, and after drying, is used as fuel or converted into trinboard, used in construction.

Lime is added to the extracted juice, and the mixture is boiled to remove impurities, which form compounds with the lime. The resulting juice is treated for a few more impurities and then evaporated, producing a thick syrup. The syrup is spun very quickly in a centrifuge. This separates the sugar crystals from the liquid, which is known as molasses. This too is a valuable commodity. In Trinidad the molasses is used in the manufacture of rum, as food for livestock, and in the manufacture of ethyl alcohol.

The sugar crystals are treated to produce the various types of sugar. Brown sugar is produced by reintroducing molasses to the crystals. In Trinidad and Tobago most of the sugarcane estates and the factories that service the production are in the south of Trinidad. There is a large sugar mill at Couva, and the exported sugar is sent from nearby Point Lisas. A huge, state-owned refinery dominates the economy around Guayaguayare, also in the south.

TRANSPORTATION

It is a common joke in Trinidad and Tobago that although there are thousands of people employed in repairing the roads, the roads are still always full of potholes and are liable to disappear altogether. Trinidad's main transportation system is its network of roads. The islands have 4,409 miles (7,900 km) of roads, including 31 miles (50 km) of highway. Freight is transported by road in trucks. There is no navigable waterway of any consequence and no rail system. The main air route into Trinidad is via Piarco International Airport, and the chief ports are Port-of-Spain, Point Fortin, Point-à-Pierre, and Brighton as well as Point Lisas, the main industrial complex in the country.

A family outing to the beach is made convenient by the family car.

Tourists are attracted by the well-conserved natural beauty of Trinidad and Tobago. Here, a group is visiting the Caroni Bird Sanctuary.

TOURISM

Tourism is the country's fourth largest foreign exchange earner and is growing annually. Tourism is centered on the less industrially developed Tobago, with most of the beach resorts and tourist hotels concentrated there. It is served by an airport capable of taking wide bodied aircraft, and there are plans to develop a third international airport on Trinidad. Port-of-Spain on Trinidad is a major tourist destination, and most cruise ships enter the islands at Port-of-Spain Harbor. Scarborough in Tobago is another destination for tourist ships. The islands are less dependent on tourism than other Caribbean islands and so are not so susceptible to the disadvantages of the industry—cluttered beaches and damaged environment caused by inconsiderate tourists, tour buses, and excessive development of infrastructure.

Fishermen bringing in their catch at Grafton Beach, Tobago.

THE FISHING INDUSTRY

In the last 20 years, Trinidad and Tobago's fishing industry has seen changes from a series of individuals with small boats to a major industry, earning important export dollars. In 1977 the government offered financial incentives to people prepared to take up the livelihood. Now 9,000 people are in the industry. Unfortunately, the area around the islands has become overfished, and Trinidad often finds itself in dispute with neighboring Venezuela over territorial rights. The job of the navy is patrolling the waters for rogue fishermen. Trinidadians are also sometimes caught fishing illegally in Venezuelan waters. Trinidad allows the use of ghost nets—transparent plastic nets—that are banned by many other countries because of the effect it has on fish stocks. Trinidad has had a shrimp fleet since the 1970s. The shrimp is canned and processed on the island.

Fishermen bringing in their catch at Grafton Beach, Tobago.

TRINIDADIANS & TOBAGONIANS

TRINIDAD AND TOBAGO IS A TRULY MULTI-ETHNIC COUNTRY. Its ethnic mix consists of descendants of the Carib Indians who first inhabited the islands; French Creole, Spanish, and English settlers, descendants of the black slaves, Indians whose great grandparents arrived as indentured workers; Portuguese; Italians; and Chinese. In addition to these, there are the many mixed-race citizens of Trinidad whose ancestors might be a mixture of any of these other ethnic groups. When the first census of Trinidad and Tobago was taken in 1861, the population was 100,000. By 1921 it had grown to 360,000. Its current population of about 1.1 million is dominated by people of African and Indian descent. Trinidad and Tobago has a fairly average birth rate for the Caribbean, but the low infant mortality rate keeps the population growth high.

Left: **A group of friends chatting after work.**

Opposite: **A vegetable vendor taking a breather in the morning Scarborough market.**

AMERINDIANS

The very first inhabitants of the islands were Amerindians who migrated to the islands from Venezuela. Other Indian groups were the Carib and Arawak. Tobago was uninhabited when Christopher Columbus arrived. In the years of colonial exploitation, few of these people survived as a distinct culture, and almost all had been assimilated into other groups by the end of the 19th century.

EUROPEANS

The next people to arrive on the islands were Europeans, first the Spanish, then the French, and later the English, as well as small numbers of Italians and Portuguese. In the 18th and 19th centuries, these people formed the wealthy, ruling aristocratic classes of Trinidad. Their descendents still live on the old plantations inherited from the original settlers, or own and manage big businesses such as tourism, imports and exports, and banking.

AFRICANS

Several distinct groups of Africans arrived on the islands at different times. Black people tend to work in white-collar jobs, but very few are businessmen or farm workers. Many black people are doctors, nurses, teachers, lawyers, and lecturers.

MULATTOS

This is a term used in Trinidad and Tobago to describe people of mixed race. Although they may be of mixed descent, they are culturally part of the black community. But much like the coloreds in segregated South Africa, there is a small group that considers itself racially distinct and which cultivates marriages with similarly colored mulatto families.

One group of mulattos has its own name—Dougla. They are of mixed Indian and African ancestry.

INDIANS

Indians make up over 40% of the population, the largest ethnic group on Trinidad. Many of them claim a 150-year lineage on the island. Most of them are farmers who live in the rual areas; the rest are white-collar workers. Indians have moved into small businesses more extensively than people of African descent. Many people of Indian descent have retained their religion and culture, although it has been altered by European and African influences. They are Hindu, Muslim, and Christian by religion. Indian people tend to live as extended families, with several generations of one family living together.

An East Indian wedding. Both bride and groom are in elaborate traditional costumes and headwear.

CHINESE AND LEBANESE

Scattered throughout the world as traders, the Chinese and Lebanese have a strong presence in the chief towns of Trinidad and Tobago, and the Chinese often run the small shops in the villages. Chinese genes have entered into the ethnic mix of Trinidad, and there are many people who have Chinese blood as well as African and Indian.

INTERETHNIC RELATIONS

Diverse as Trinidad and Tobago's population is, the various ethnic groups do not mix freely. At the top of the social hierarchy are the white, descendants of the early settlers, American businessmen, Chinese businessmen, and the Lebanese. Below them on the social scale are the educated middle-class blacks and ethnic-Indians and businessmen, and both groups tend to remain apart. There is also little contact between these people and the higher classes.

The sense of community among the various ethnic groups is not strong, although there is a vibrant diversity in Trinidadian society.

53

LIFESTYLE

FOR THE PEOPLE OF TRINIDAD AND TOBAGO, there are common elements of lifestyle—the climate, economic and physical conditions, life expectancy, education, health care—but for each of the ethnic groups that live on the islands, there are cultural differences, as well as political divisions that keep them apart.

In Trinidad and Tobago there is very little of the uglier aspects of racism. The various cultural groups have intermarried and at times such as Carnival, they enjoy a common activity. There is also none of the avoidance of racial matters in Trinidad and Tobago that gets labeled as discrimination in Western countries. Trinidadians in particular will discuss skin tone and racial characteristics in a way that more sophisticated societies do not.

Left: **Muslim girls on their way to religious school.**

Opposite: **Children enjoying themselves after school is out.**

A relaxed lifestyle characterizes the culture of the blacks.

BLACK LIFESTYLE

Black people make up the largest ethnic group in Trinidad and Tobago. They are united by their ethnicity and common heritage. Their ancestors arrived on the islands as slaves, either directly in slave ships which had bought them from the west coast of Africa, often Ghana, or as slaves of settlers from other Caribbean islands. If all black people in Trinidad and Tobago have a common outlook on life, it is a laidback one. Characteristic is Carnival, which evolved among the black people of Trinidad as an irreverent and often outrageous celebration.

The diversity of languages and religions that the slaves brought with them to the islands meant that a common tongue and way of life had to evolve. It was black slaves who created the use of pidgin, which has influenced Trinidad English, because they had no common language to share.

Many aspects of African life have remained but in a highly evolved way. African religions have influenced Trinidad's religions, and the rhythms of African music can be heard in the counterpoint rhythms of

Carnival. Most black people left the countryside after emancipation. This group is chiefly urban and has received a good education. Their religions are often new forms of Christianity, and there are large numbers of Rastafarians. During the 1970s and the upsurge in black power movements in the United States, a particular style of dressing emerged with Afro hairstyles and loose, brightly patterned African shirts. Today, however, men wear casual T-shirts and slacks in their leisure time. For the office, a tie and short-sleeved shirt are more common. Black people tend to work in white-collar jobs, and for many years, they dominated the civil service. Black households often diverge from the standard married couple and children of the nuclear family.

A typical black household may be made up of either a couple living together, or a family headed by only a mother.

LIFE IN THE CITY

Trinidad and Tobago has only two cities, Port-of-Spain and San Fernando. Both are on Trinidad. Business hours in these two cities are a little longer than in most European cities, from 8 a.m. to 6:30 p.m., and stores stay open late in the evening and on the weekend. Port-of-Spain is the administrative center of the islands, and many civil service workers live there. Besides administration and banking, Port-of-Spain is an industrial base with many of its citizens working in sawmills, textile mills, citrus canneries, and the Angostura bitters factory. The city has a major port, and part of the University of the West Indies is close by. San Fernando is located in the oil fields, and most of the people work in the oil industry.

City life in Trinidad is filled with color and vibrant activities.

CITY HOMES

In the cities most people live in wooden houses. In the suburbs of Port-of-Spain, these homes seem to disappear into the hills behind the city where houses perch in steeply sloping yards. Houses are small, often one-story buildings with corrugated iron roofs, but they are in shady suburbs lined with fruit trees and have clean running water and a constant supply of electricity. As people have grown wealthier, they have added on more stories to their houses, which take on a strange, impromptu form as they expand upward. Individual suburbs were developed for the various ethnic groups and are still largely racially divided. Huge brick houses, built in many different styles, stand out among the simpler buildings. Most of them are in the center of cities like Port-of-Spain and are still privately owned or have become government offices.

Trinidadians and Tobagonians often shop in sophisticated malls where expensive imported clothes and electrical goods are displayed in Western-style department stores.

Houses built on slope and plains enjoy the advantages of space and creative style compared to city homes.

MARKETS

While Trinidad and Tobago has a fair share of supermarkets where people go to buy expensive imports from the United States, it also has flourishing street markets where people can buy fresh local produce. Fruit stalls line the streets of the cities, and at the harbors, every kind of fish is laid out on stalls for sale. While some of the street markets are highly regulated, covered markets, others are little shanty towns where the vendors have built rickety buildings along the street or inside unused building sites. Many of the stallholders actually live on the premises, and small villages have sprung up within the city populated by the stallholders. Craft markets also spring up in tourist areas selling Rastafarian T-shirts and locally made basketware at quite high prices. Cooked food stalls also line the streets, selling ready-made Chinese, Indian, and Trinidadian meals to office workers.

Sisters selling shoes and an old gas pump from a van.

INDIAN LIFESTYLE

For a hundred years or more, the Indian population of Trinidad and Tobago was poorly educated field workers, but as education has improved in the last 20 years or so, a demographic change has been taking place, with Indians moving into middle-class, white-collar jobs and into the cities to work.

Because of their origin, many Indian families have retained ties with their ancestral country. Black people arrived in Trinidad and Tobago, most of them unwillingly, because they had been kidnapped in their native home in Africa and taken away from people who shared their languages and customs. Indian people arrived voluntarily, perhaps with friends, and were able to write to family back home. Many Indian businessmen still have ties with their families in India, and as in many other expatriate communities, customs have been fiercely retained in a way that might have slackened a little in the home country.

Hindu women at a local festive celebration. They are wearing the traditional Indian dress—the sari.

LIFE IN THE COUNTRY

The thirty-nine percent of the population of Trinidad and Tobago that lives in the country is mostly located in the south of Trinidad where there are still large sugar plantations, or in the west of the island around Arouca. Some of them live in Tobago, which has virtually no big industries. The rural folks in Tobago either farm or work in the tourism industry or for local government.

Life on the big estates is hard, and most estate workers are poor. Most people live in small, single-story wooden houses with tin roofs and often a large overhanging veranda to keep off the sun. They supplement their income with their own fruit and vegetable gardens. There are amenities of modern life at the estate houses, but many of the sugarcane workers belong to an organization called Sou-sou Land Limited which buys land to develop on behalf of the poor and landless. The poor literally put all their excess cash into savings with the company until they have enough to buy some of its land.

LIFE IN TOBAGO

If Trinidad is busy, noisy, polluted in places, and full of congested roads, Tobago is slow and easygoing, with tiny villages dotted around the countryside, and the majority of people employed on their own small farms or in tourism. Buildings are all small-scale—pretty, bungalow-style cottages, some of them the expensive country homes of wealthy Trinidadians and others more modest homes of the local people. Roads are narrow and largely unpaved and some disappear in a bad rainy season. This does not mean that Tobago does not have the dynamic energy of Trinidad—Tobago has its own Carnival and many rural festivals that are celebrated with style and pomp. Most of these festivals are Christian in origin. The only town of any size on Tobago is Scarborough and this resembles a small country town in Europe rather than a thriving capital city.

Shopping along the streets of Scarborough.

EDUCATION AND HEALTH

Nearly 98% of the total population 15 years and above has received an education. Education is free and compulsory between the ages of 6 and 12. There are about 500 primary schools on the islands and 100 secondary schools. Attendance in secondary school has risen from 42% of the relevant age group in 1972 to 76% in the late 1990s. Secondary education is based on the old British system, where an examination taken at age 11 draws out the top students to grammar schools, while those who do not pass the test attend a secondary school where the emphasis is on technical subjects. While education facilities expanded significantly during the boom years of the 1970s, there are still very large class sizes and more children seeking a higher education than places available. There are three campuses of the University of the West Indies in Trinidad and Tobago offering degree courses in engineering, law, medicine, education, agriculture, liberal arts, natural science, and social sciences. Technical colleges also provide tertiary education in Port-of-Spain,

Centeno, and San Fernando. There are several teacher training colleges. Wealthier students who can afford the fees tend to go to university in the United States. Some private schools are run by Christian groups. Adult literacy is around 98% of the population. Statistics have shown that 301 out of a thousand people own a television set; 188 out of a thousand a car; 174 out of a thousand a telephone.

The infant mortality rate in Trinidad and Tobago is 13 per thousand live births, a better average than most Caribbean countries. There is one doctor per 1,213 people. Life expectancy is around 72 years, also, very high for the region. Major causes of death are cerebrovascular and heart disease, cancer, and diabetes. The government runs a national health care program as well as a compulsory retirement pension plan, and there are benefits for maternity leave, sickness, and industrial injury. About 20% of the population lives below the poverty line.

Automatic 24-hour bank tellers are commonly found in the streets of the city.

TRANSPORTATION

Trinidad once had a railway line, but it was closed down in the mid-20th century. Most people get about the islands by road in their own, often ramshackle cars or by using the public buses or maxi-taxis. These are official taxis that travel certain routes stopping on request. The taxi driver picks up passengers, negotiates a fare, and gives change from money he holds in his hand, all the while maneuvering along some very sharp mountain passes. The taxis are often air-conditioned and well looked-after since their owners spend most of their day in them. Loud calypso music dominates, and the passengers will often argue loudly about politics or music or some other hot topic.

Besides the maxi-taxis, there are regular single-fare taxis, but these are for tourists or the rich. Many local taxis are not registered and are just owned by someone out to make a bit of extra cash. Trinidad and Tobago's local airlines tend to be equally casual—the flights are short, and passengers tend to carry quite a lot of unusual hand baggage.

Since only one-fifth of the population owns a car, other means of transportation are fairly common. Ox carts and buffalo carts travel the rural roads carrying people and farm produce, bicycles roam everywhere, and in some places, the beach provides the main route in and out of town.

White vans with red stripes, called taxis, are one of the major forms of public transportation.

WEDDINGS

In the black community of Trinidad and Tobago, Christianity is the predominant religion and couples often prefer a traditional-style wedding, with the bride in a white dress and the groom in a black suit.

Hindu weddings are traditional. Marriages are arranged between families, usually with someone of the same caste. The bride and groom meet a few times before the wedding, then do not meet at all in the days before the wedding.

THE WHITE LIFESTYLE

White citizens of Trinidad and Tobago have lives that are very distant from the ordinary people. Their children attend private schools run by the religious orders and they live in large private estates in the countryside. Their leisure activities separate them from ordinary Trinidadians and Tobagonians as do their jobs, which are in the higher management.

The Trinidadian wedding is usually Westernized, with a white bridal gown, flower girls, and a garden reception.

RELIGION

MOST PEOPLE IN TRINIDAD AND TOBAGO practice a religion, with each ethnic group practicing its own religion. Among the whites are the traditional European religions of Roman Catholicism (32.2% of the total population) and Anglicanism (14.4 % of the total population). Many black Trinidadians are also Christians, but they practice more recent forms of Christianity, such as Seventh Day Adventism, Methodism, and Pentecostalism. Other blacks are Rastafarians. Among the Indian population are Hindus (24.3% of the total population) and Shiite Muslims (6% of the total population), and the small Chinese community practices a mixture of Buddhism and Taoism. A small black Muslim community exists but is entirely separate from the Asian Muslim community.

Left: **A street vendor in Scarborough selling incense and other items used for worship.**

Opposite: **One of the many majestic Catholic cathedrals that are more modern than colonial in style.**

The name "Shouter" of the Shouter Baptism faith comes from practicioners' tendency to stand in public places proclaiming their faith.

ORISHA

The slaves who came to Trinidad brought with them elements of their original African religious beliefs. In Trinidad these beliefs became mixed with a Christian faith. Most people of African descent practice the Shango or Orisha, a religion largely found in Tobago. In this form of worship, participants believe that besides an all-powerful God, there are spirits that exist in everything around them. This belief is known as animism. In order to pacify and even to get help from these spirits, one must worship them through ritual dances, offerings, chanting, singing, and prayer.

Orisha originated among the Yoruba, an African people who once inhabited an area from Benin to the Niger River but who now live largely in Nigeria. During British rule in Trinidad and Tobago, the religion was suppressed and thus its practice became secretive, and it remains so today. The most notable animist god is Shango, the god of thunder, fire, war, and drumming, who is depicted carrying an axe. The religion remains Christian, however, since Shango is associated with a Christian saint—St. Barbara. Another of the deities of the Orisha religion is Ogun, who is the god of blacksmiths.

Orisha worship takes place in a *palais*, which is often a sheltered courtyard partly covered by a galvanized roof and decorated with ritual objects such as weapons, jugs, and the materials used during worship such as wine or oil.

SPIRITUAL BAPTISTS

Another form of worship banned by the British, Spiritual Baptism, is a form of Christianity that came to the islands in the 19th century. The religion was officially banned in 1917. The ban was lifted on

March 30, 1951, which the Spiritual Baptists celebrate as Shouter Baptist Liberation Day.

The basis of the faith is the worship of the Holy Trinity—Father, Son, and Holy Ghost—but like Orisha, this faith recognizes animist spirits, that must be placated. Outwardly, the Shouter Baptist church looks like any other Christian church with an altar and rows of pews. But these churches include a center pole from which are hung symbolic objects used to call up the animist spirits. Members of the church dress up on Sundays in long white robes and colorful headgear and attend services that can last up to six hours. The service begins by casting out any unpleasant spirits known as *jumbies* ("JUM-bees") that might be in the church. Lighted candles are placed at strategic places, incense is burned, and brass bells are rung. The service proceeds with readings from the Bible to the rhythmic clapping of hands. Like followers of Orisha, members of the congregation become possessed by spirits and shout out loud, often speaking in tongues, that is, in another, unfamiliar language.

Shouter Baptists in Scarborough preaching through the ringing of bells.

71

RASTAFARIANS

This religion, which originated in Jamaica, has become very popular in Trinidad in recent years. It is a Christian-based religion that follows certain texts of the Bible. Rastafarians believe that the late Emperor of Ethiopia, Haile Selassie ("HIGH-lee se-LASS-ee") is God. Their name for God is Jah. They believe the emperor was the 225th incarnation of King Solomon, which makes him a modern messiah. In addition, Rastafarians do not eat processed food, salt, meat, or dairy products, and may not use any stimulants, although marijuana is used during prayer meetings or meditation. Some of those practicing the religion believe that all black people should return to Ethiopia. Rastafarians typically wear long dreadlocks in keeping with the Bible's exhortation, "They shall not make baldness upon their head, neither shall they shave off the corner of their beard."

HINDUISM

Hinduism was introduced to Trinidad and Tobago by the Indian indentured workers, but after 150 years, it has changed quite a lot from the religion practiced in India.

Hinduism is polytheistic—Hindus worship a pantheon of gods. At the head of the pantheon is Shiva, the god of creation and destruction. He is depicted with snakes for hair and a third eye on his forehead and riding a bull. Next in importance is Vishnu, multi-armed and blue, who is said to be the angel of deliverance. Believers think he will appear on earth one day and punish the wicked and deliver the pure to heaven. Ganesh, the

Devotees outside a Hindu temple, which is dotted with sculptures of the Hindu gods along its corridor.

elephant-headed god, is the god of education and literature. Lakshmi is the goddess of light and prosperity who is worshipped at the Diwali festival. Other gods are Durga, wife of Shiva, depicted wearing a necklace of skulls with blood dripping from her mouth; Saraswati, the goddess of purification; and Hanuman, the demon fighter who invented Sanskrit.

Unlike Hinduism in India, the version in Trinidad and Tobago has almost no vestige of the caste system. In India people marry and accept employment within their caste, but in the islands the only sign of the caste system are the Brahmins of the priestly caste or pundits.

A Hindu religious service in the islands is also different from those in India. The service takes place in the temple as it would in India, but the service, called a *puja* ("PU-ja"), combines worship of several deities at once; in India the *puja* is dedicated to only one deity. During the service, the priest arranges votive offerings such as flowers, food, oil, herbs, and pictures of the deity. Then the pundit blesses the arrangements and anoints a flagpole. The deities' flags are hoisted, symbolizing the blessing of the building and the participants.

Hindus in Trinidad and Tobago celebrate Diwali, the Festival of Lights, and Phagwa, the spring festival.

ISLAM

This religion originated in seventh-century Arabia through the prophet Mohammed. Its followers are known as Muslims, and the religion is comprehensive, covering almost every aspect of their lives. It is based on the five pillars of wisdom: the creed, performance of prayer, giving of alms, observance of fasting, and a pilgrimage to Mecca.

The creed can be summed up by the words: there is no God but God and Mohammed is the prophet of God. There are 28 other prophets, including Christ, but Mohammed is the most important.

Muslims must pray at least five times a day: at sunrise, noon, late afternoon, sunset, and before bed. A distinctive architectural feature of mosques all over the world as well as in Trinidad and Tobago is the minaret. This is where the muezzin calls the worshippers to prayer.

Left: **The Crown Point Mosque in Tobago is one of the places of worship for Muslims in the city.**

Opposite: **A female Hindu saying prayers to a god.**

Muslims are expected to give 2.5% of their annual salary to the poor. During the holy month of Ramadan, no food or drink or tobacco may be consumed between sunrise and sunset. Children begin to take part in the annual fast at about age 9. The fifth pillar of the faith is the pilgrimage to Mecca that all Muslims are expected to complete at least once in their life. There is an unwritten sixth pillar of the faith, the *jihad* ("JEE-had") or holy war against the unfaithful.

Most Muslims in Trinidad and Tobago are Shiite. This sect traces its origins back to the time when Ali, the son-in-law and nephew of the prophet Mohammed, was murdered. Followers of the religion were called Shi'I, meaning followers of Ali, and this has come to be Shiite.

Muslim men gathered for worship and study of the Koran.

SUPERSTITIONS AND TRADITIONAL BELIEFS

Many people in Trinidad and Tobago, not just black people, believe in black magic. *Jumbies* ("JUM-bees"), or *dih* ("DEE") to the Indians, come in many forms. *Douens* ("DOO-ens") are the spirits of unbaptized children and are malevolent. Their faces have no features and their feet point backwards, so they are easily recognized. People who believe in these spirits seldom speak their children's names aloud for fear that the *douens* might learn them and harm the children.

The *lugarhoo* ("LOO-gar-who") feeds on fresh blood and drags iron chains behind it so it can be heard coming. It can change shape, so superstitious people often hang over the bed a pair of open scissors in the shape of the crucifix to ward off the *lugarhoo*.

A *soucouyant* ("SUE-koo-ant") is a female vampire that takes the form of an old woman and lives among the people. She travels around as a ball of fire, keeping her skin in a container while she flies. If the skin is found, covering it in salt is supposed to prevent her from getting back into it.

Among the Carib population, there is a story that explains the origin of the pitch lake. Once, the story goes, the Chiman tribe lived on the site of

TRADITIONAL MEDICINE

Part of the African religious traditions in Trinidad and especially in Tobago is a system of natural medicine. Herbal medicines are dispensed by the *obeah* ("OH-bee-a"), but many people know the use of natural herbal remedies. Typical of this kind of medicine is the bush bath. The *obeah* selects particular herbs and other remedies and boils them. The infusion is drunk. The herbs must be collected at a certain time depending on the ailment. The cures can be for physical illnesses or psychic ones. Some herbs are cooling, while others are purging. Purging herbs are senna, pawpaw bark, or castor oil. For colds everyone knows the use of lemon grass, black sage, and Christmas bush. Fevers are treated with lime and St. John's bush, while Tia Marie leaves cure insomnia.

the lake. At that time, the lake did not exist and the surrounding countryside was fertile and beautiful. The Chiman had a wonderful life, but they became too vain. They began to hunt hummingbirds, which were protected by the gods. In retribution, the gods created the pitch lake and buried all the Chiman tribe beneath it.

Another legend tells of the origin of Mount Naparima, which is thought to be the body of Haburi, an Indian hero.

In Tobago there is a particularly ferocious story about Mamoo Brebna, who was an African slave. He was so powerful that he was able to stop the sugar mills from working, and when his master tried to beat him, the master's wife felt the pain.

The hummingbird, which the Caribs believed to be protected by the gods and which was hunted by the Chiman tribe.

CATHOLICISM AND ANGLICANISM

There are many forms of Christianity in Trinidad and Tobago. Christianity is the official religion, and the predominant form is Roman Catholicism. The tenets of Roman Catholicism are the belief in the Holy Trinity; the veneration of Mary, the mother of Jesus; and the belief in transubstantiation: during the Catholic Mass, the priest performs a ritual in which the communion wafer and wine, through a miracle, "become" the body and blood of Christ. The Anglican church is very close in ideology and ritual to Roman Catholicism. Both have ornately decorated churches and in both the priesthood determines church policy, although Anglicans do not recognize the Pope. Also, Holy Communion is treated as simply a symbol of the body and blood of Christ. In both churches worship takes place on Sundays, and in Trinidad and Tobago both religions are practiced chiefly by the white minority. Another Christian denomination, the Presbyterian church, originated in Scotland and is governed by a body of laymen.

The design of the Church of the Sacred Heart marries Catholic and Anglican traditions.

LANGUAGE

TRINIDAD AND TOBAGO'S OFFICIAL LANGUAGE IS ENGLISH, but many visitors to the country might have considerable trouble recognizing the language spoken on the streets. In official circles, standard English is the norm, and the more highly educated a person, the closer the dialect will be to standard English. But in casual conversation and in most informal situations, everybody, including the white elite, uses Trini, a form of English based a little on the many languages that have been fed into the culture.

THE FIRST CREOLE

When African slaves were first brought to Trinidad and Tobago, they spoke a multitude of African languages, depending on their place of origin

Left: **A loud and bold advertisement in English flanks the door of a restaurant.**

Opposite: **A big sign at the entrance to a newly opened shopping center.**

A group of friends chatting.

in Africa. In order to communicate with each other and to take orders from their masters, they had to find a lingua franca, a common language that they could all understand. From this need emerged a Creole language, based loosely on English but incorporating many African words and expressions. The grammar at first was probably African with English nouns added as a common core of understanding. Each African spoke his or her own language fluently and perhaps a little bit of the other slaves' languages as well, but all their orders came in French, Spanish, or English. Therefore, over generations, the African languages gave way to the languages of the slave masters, and the mother tongue of the slaves became a hybridized language or pidgin.

For about a hundred years, the language spoken in Trinidad and Tobago was a pidgin form of French, which was basically French with Twi or Yoruba words included. Even today, there is a strong element of French in Trini, and in some rural areas, people still speak a language that is closer to French than to English.

THE FRENCH INFLUENCE

There are many French expressions and words in Trini. Most of the words that describe the *jumbies* of superstition are of French derivation. Also, many words for plants are French in origin. If someone spreads spiteful gossip about a neighbor, it is called *mauvais-langue* (bad language). The French influence is even more noticeable in Trini syntax. In French, describing the weather involves the verb *faire*, "to do" or "to make," so that a French person would say *Il fait brillait*—the weather is fine. In Trini, French words are directly translated into English, but the structure remains French so that a Trinidadian might say "It making hot" instead of "It is hot."

A vegetable vendor talking to her customer.

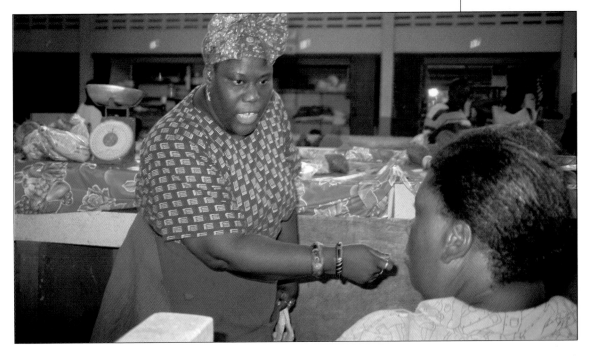

HINDI

The Indian workers who came to Trinidad and Tobago were different from the African slaves, as they came with a common culture and language and maintained their own language as indentured workers. Hindi, the language that most of them spoke, is still used in the Indian community, although it is rarely spoken in the workplace or at mixed social events. Younger people tend to be more fluent with Trini or standard English.

Most of the indentured workers lived in specific rural areas of Trinidad and still make up a large portion of the community in the south and east of the island. It is possible to see the continuing development of Trini as a language in the way that Hindi has influenced the Creole spoken in Trinidad. Indian workers are still largely associated with smallholdings as vegetable growers, so many of the words for vegetables have two options—one the older English, French, or Spanish word and the other a newer, Hindi one. In Trinidad and Tobago the bulbous, purple vegetable that Americans call an eggplant is known as *melongene* from an early French word. Now it is also called *beigun* from Hindi. English speakers call it aubergine.

TRINI

The language spoken in Trinidad and Tobago is a mixture of influences from other languages, and it is still changing. In Tobago there have been fewer influences, so the language has fewer Hindi additions and is a closer mix of African and English languages. But Trini is not just a collection of borrowed nouns and a few odd phrases. It has a special quality of its own that reflects the national character. Trini, for example, uses many more double entendres than British or American English. One explanation for this manner of saying one thing but meaning another is that during slavery, the slaves had to be careful of what they said in front of their masters and so developed this way of speaking.

Opposite: **Most Indian shop owners speak Hindi to their Indian counterparts but English to other customers.**

A TRINI GLOSSARY

Many of the expressions peculiar to Trinidad and Tobago are connected with having fun, relaxing, enjoying Carnival, and other aspects of social life. In businesses and schools, standard English is used, so it is only on the streets that the really colorful sayings can be heard. Here are some of them.

bashment	a big party or a festival that went really well
beastly	very cold beer
big up	bragging and praising someone else at the same time
boldfaced	being pushy, promoting yourself
break a lime	leaving a party when it is at its height
darkers	sunglasses
dou dou	sweetheart
ignorant	quick to take offense
jammin	working hard
liming	having a good time with your friends
sweetman	a man who is supported by his girlfriend
Tobago love	not showing your real feelings

THE MEDIA

Trinidad has two daily broadsheet newspapers, the conservative *Trinidad Guardian* and the more liberal *Independent*. More popular and widely read are the tabloid daily newspapers, which are photograph-oriented and full of local gossip, the *Express* and *Newsday*. Also popular are the evening newspapers, the *Sun* and the *Evening News*. All of these papers have large weekend versions full of color supplements, arts sections, sports sections, and cartoons, but more popular than any of these on the weekends are the scandal sheets—*Bomb*, *Blast*, *Heat*, and *Sunday Punch*, which are full of gossip, pictures of scantily clad women, and huge, shocking headlines.

Trinidadians having a ball at a concert. With better access to information through the country's developing media, more and more young people become familiar with Western pop culture.

In Tobago the single paper is *Tobago News*, published on Fridays, so most Tobagonians read the Trinidad papers. Trinidadians and Tobagonians are also fond of foreign magazines, which are readily available in the cities. Trinidad produces two glossy magazines of its own, *Ibis*, which focuses on local cultural events, and *Esse*, a woman's magazine.

Television is not as ubiquitous in Trinidad and Tobago as in the United States; only about one-eighth of the population owns a television. There are three terrestrial TV channels, the state-owned TTT station, and two commercial channels. Popular programs include American soaps such as *the Bold and the Beautiful*, situation comedies, American game shows, and lots of music programs that focus on local music and musicians, particularly late at night when there are live broadcasts. Most set owners also have access to cable TV where many American channels such as CNN, Discovery, and HBO broadcast directly into the home. American television programs are also available via satellite.

Radio is more popular than television. The best radio caters to local taste with talk shows and news about big parties and upcoming fetes. Music stations broadcast almost nonstop calypso between November and February before the annual calypso competition, after which the airwaves resound to the music of reggae. There are about 14 Trinidad-based radio stations, one dedicated entirely to Indian movie music and Indian reggae, three to popular music and talk, and several for classical and middle-of-the-road music.

A girl listening to music on the radio. Stations offer a good mix of Indian and African-American music for fans of any ethnic and age group—the essence of a vibrant multiethnic culture.

ARTS

THE RICH CULTURE OF TRINIDAD AND TOBAGO manifests itself in a variety of artistic forms, but music is unquestionably the most vibrant and influential way that people of the two islands express themselves.

STEEL SOUNDS

The steel band is one of the country's most distinctive contributions to world music, and it reflects the talent of ordinary people who may not be able to read a musical score but who are nonetheless able to play an astonishing variety of different types of music. This variety extends from internationally-recognized classical pieces by composers like Mozart to contemporary music written for and by working-class musicians who seek to comment on social and political life.

Left: **The steel drum, the pan, has the distinction of being the only new acoustic instrument of the 20th century.**

Opposite: **A sculpture at the entrance of the museum in Tobago.**

The steel drum, more commonly known as the pan, is the defining instrument of the steel band. Its well-documented origin goes back to the 1930s when empty oil drums were first used instead of the bottles, garbage can lids, and other materials that had been used by percussion musicians too poor to afford anything else.

PARANG

The music of Trinidad and Tobago is a synthesis of African and European musical traditions that has its origins in the arrival of Spanish colonizers at the end of the 15th century. The Spanish introduced Christmas carols, and today, the legacy of this can be heard in traditional Christmas music known as *parang* ("par-ANG"). This kind of music is heard throughout the month of December and into January, and the musicians are known as *parranderos* ("par-an-DARE-owes").

A group of singers performing to an enthusiastic audience.

THE MIGHTY SPARROW

One of the figures most closely associated with the rich talent produced
by the craze for calypso is a musician who was never called simply by his
surname, which is Sparrow, but always by the epithet of Mighty Sparrow.
He first emerged in the 1950s and his musical abilities coincided with the
growing popularity of the long-playing record (LP). This allowed musicians
with the necessary talent to develop a repertoire of pieces that could make
up the extended number of tracks that the LP allowed. Until the advent of
the LP, a band would release just two tracks, one on each side of the short-
playing record. Sparrow produced his first LP in 1957, and with his own
recording company, he went on to regularly release an album each year.
When the new government established by Eric Williams in 1956 introduced
the Calypso King musical competition, the Mighty Sparrow won.

Three boys performing at the Carnival celebration in Port-of-Spain.

CALYPSO MEETS DISCO POP

By the late 1970s, it seemed to some musicians that calypso was losing its verve, especially in the face of competition from the growing globalization of pop and disco music. Rather than die a slow death, calypso bounced back with a vengeance and the new sound was christened soca.

The musician most closely associated with the birth of soca is Lord Shorty or, as he is now known, Ras Shorty I. He sped up the tempo of calypso and made it more compatible with the funky dance music that was sweeping across the United States. The synthesizers and other electronic aids to musical composition that were fuelling the disco craze also found a place in the rejuvenated calypso sound.

Soca is currently the most popular form of calypso music in Trinidad and Tobago, and it dominates the big festivals, especially Carnival. There

Limbo dancing is often performed for tourists in the resorts.

is now a well-established annual competition that, echoing the Calypso King event, awards the title of the Soca Monarch to the victor. Super Blue, Chinese Laundry, KMC, and Tony Prescott are currently some of the most popular soca musicians. Their new releases are eagerly awaited by the public.

Not to be left behind by the trend, Indians have evolved their own version of soca. It carries the delightful appellation of chutney soca. This is a unique musical form and is evidence of the astonishing richness and creativity of cultural life in Trinidad and Tobago. Chutney soca displays the same fast-paced tempo of traditional soca but married to and merging with the sound of sitars and Hindi and English lyrics. The synthesis is mirrored in the dance movements of chutney soca, which manage to combine the gusto of calypso dancing with the highly formalized hand and arm movements of classical Indian dance.

A more serious and meaningful message, "Say no to drugs," underlies the colorful banner.

LITERATURE

The creative and imaginative use of language as an art form does more than make itself felt in the clever lyrics and verbal puns that form so essential a part of the musical tradition of calypso. The country's literary tradition can be traced back to at least the 1930s when a diverse group of young writers began to experiment with different literary forms. Short stories and poems began to appear in print, and soon the first novels made their appearance.

After World War II, Samuel Selvon, a local writer, made an impact with his humorous novel *A Brighter Sun*, and this was followed by the more gritty *The Lonely Londoners*. This novel, set in London in the postwar era, told the sad reality of the racism that immigrants from Trinidad and Tobago often encountered when they came to Britain to start a new life. Equally influential has been the work of Earl Lovelace, especially his powerful novel *The Dragon Can't Dance*, which explores the phenomenon of Carnival.

Alongside the novelist V.S. Naipul, the local poet Derek Walcott has achieved the most in establishing the international renown of Trinidadian literature. Walcott was born in 1930 on the island of St. Lucia, but after studying at a university in Jamaica, he moved to Trinidad where he became a journalist and lived for decades. He published poetry and plays, and in 1957 went to New York to study theater. Two years later he founded and directed the Trinidad Theater Workshop and out of this artistic venture, there emerged a number of talented actors. In 1992 Walcot was awarded the Nobel Prize for Literature, the most prestigious literary award in the world.

Children attending English class in school.

V.S. NAIPUL

The novelist whose work and influence has made itself most powerfully felt around the world is V.S. Naipul. He was born in 1932 into a family that had emigrated from India. His father was a noted journalist who also published a collection of short stories. Naipul did well at school and won a scholarship that took him to Oxford University in England where he studied literature. His first novels appeared in the 1950s, but it was the publication of *A House for Mr. Biswas* in 1961 that established his fame as a writer. After traveling through the Caribbean, he published *The Middle Passage* in 1961 and expressed the view that the West Indies was a home to displaced people who did not have their own cultural identity. This point of view, and his exposure of the corrupting effect of colonialism in places like Trinidad, did not always endear him to establishment figures in his country.

DEREK WALCOTT

Derek Walcott is another famous writer in Trinidad and Tobago. In 1962 Walcott brought out a collection of his poetry, entitled *In a Green Night: Poems 1948-1960,* and like much of his early work, the poems proclaimed with affection the natural beauty of the West Indies. Walcott's work examines the predicament of coming from a black culture and yet being influenced by a mainstream European culture. Many of his poems in *The Gulf* (1969) express his personal sense of alienation in being caught between two very different cultures. In *Midsummer* (1984), Walcott also explores the experience of being a black writer in the United States and the way this affects his view of his own Caribbean background.

Walcott has also written a number of plays. Those most often produced on stage are *Dream on Monkey Mountain* and *Pantomine*. His most recent poetic work is *Omeros*, hailed by many critics as one of the most significant works of Caribbean literature. The poem takes its inspiration from the ancient Greek epic of Homer's *Odyssey* and uses this tale of a man trying to return home as an extended metaphor for the plight of West Indians who also find themselves cut off from their own cultural and spiritual homeland.

VISUAL ARTS

The literary and oral tradition is so well developed in Trinidad and Tobago that the visual arts are usually relegated to a role of secondary importance in the arts. This is hardly fair because the roots of the islands' visual culture go back as far as the oral tradition and are very much a part of everyday cultural life. The best expression of the inventive and highly creative imagination of the islands' visual art is found in the rich variety of designs and motifs created for the multitude of Carnival bands. These designs call upon a number of artistic skills, like copper beating and the dextrous use of fiberglass molds, as well as a flair for eye-catching and sometimes outrageous motifs.

An artistic mural in Scarborough, Tobago.

LEISURE

THE PEOPLE OF TRINIDAD AND TOBAGO revel in their leisure time. There is a whole vocabulary of Trini English dedicated solely to the topic of leisure, especially things connected with the great festival of Carnival. Having a good time with your friends in Trinidad and Tobago is better known locally as "liming," and there is a whole set of rules about how to lime successfully.

Besides hanging out with their friends, the people of the islands also enjoy many other pursuits. Sports, such as football, golf, and water activities, are extremely popular, and the beaches and city parks are excellent places for these activities. In addition, technology also affects people's lives, providing entertainment such as soaps, documentaries, and movies on television, as well as news and music on the radio.

Left and opposite: **Work and leisure are seldom separate in the minds of Trinidadians and Tobagonians, who approach work with a relaxed attitude. These photos show co-workers chatting and having fun.**

LIMING

Liming is an activity that particularly appeals in Trinidad. It has no particular structure to it. Liming can take place in someone's home, on the beach, on the street, or at a calypso performance. A good limer has lots of time to spend and knows how to appreciate doing nothing. A typical lime might be hanging outside a department store, in the park, or in someone's yard. Leaving a liming session when it is going really well, "breaking a lime," is a bad social gaffe. When someone does this, it reminds all the other limers that they also have something to do and that they also ought to leave. This is bad for the party, and so the accusation of breaking a lime is a particularly bad one.

Liming is also taking a stroll in the streets or going shopping.

CALYPSO

Calypso is not just a musical form in Trinidad and Tobago, it is a way of life. Calypso is on the radio every day and is a powerful form of social criticism. In the islands, people spend much of their leisure time discussing the latest calypso song and analyzing the lyrics, which can often be obscure to someone who does not follow the political scene. Calypso is known as the poor people's newspaper, and songs often say obscurely things that would lead to libel actions if they were said by a politician.

Every year in Trinidad, there is a calypso competition. Long before the event begins, calypso players set up huge marquee tents in which to practice. Anyone can join the players in their tents and listen to their music.

A calypso singer encourages a tourist to listen to his performance in the calypso tents.

Trinidadians enjoying an open-air concert.

OPEN-AIR CONCERTS

When the calypso season is over, young people like to spend the summer listening to reggae and rapso music. This is played widely on the radio, but there are also large open-air concerts where well-known and lesser known reggae and rapso artists perform. The concert might take place in one of the city's parks with a deejay playing lots of music from Jamaica as well as local bands performing live. Rapso is the Trinidad and Tobago form of reggae and involves African drum beats and spoken lyrics, often of a political nature. Young people will happily spend the night and early hours dancing to local bands. These big parties or concerts are known locally as *fetes* ("FETS").

Nightclubs are also very popular after work and especially on the weekends. They open late, at about 10 p.m., and their closing times usually specify "till," which means they are open till the last person has gone home. Nightclubs are usually out of town and more sophisticated and expensive than fetes.

Early birds visiting a shopping mall before the crowds arrive.

DRUGS

Like many countries, Trinidad and Tobago has a drug scene. Although drugs, including marijuana, are illegal, people are regularly arrested for using cannabis. There is a strong counter-culture of people who use marijuana in order to lime or hang out with their friends, but it is not done openly.

SHOPPING

Trinidad in particular is full of shopping malls dedicated to American and European designer clothes. In the 1970s, during the oil boom, there was a general feeling of wealth, and many people flew to the United States for a weekend's shopping. Recently the poorer economic climate has reduced this activity. But Trinidadians love to shop, even if only to look at the goods being offered. Shopping extends also to the little stores and stalls on the streets, and a great deal of liming can take place during a shopping trip when friends meet outside a store or on the street.

A young Trinidadian learns the techniques of soccer from his more experienced friends.

SPORTS

The national pastime of Trinidad and Tobago is cricket. Most parks have several cricket pitches, and small cricket matches are set up on the streets by children. Cricket is a game most common to the British Commonwealth countries, and its rules are very complex. Cricket matches often take days to play.

In Trinidad and Tobago watching cricket as well as playing it is a favorite pastime. Most professional matches take place in March and April in Port-of-Spain. The events include very loud soca music, lots of cold drinks, and cheering on the teams when someone begins a series of runs. Much liming goes on at cricket matches.

Soccer, called football, is another game that local people, whether young or old, enjoy tremendously. When children are not playing cricket in the street, they are invariably playing soccer.

Some more expensive and elite sporting activities involve water sports such as sailing, surfing, and scuba diving around the reefs off Tobago.

DWIGHT YORKE

Dwight Yorke is one of the most successful soccer players in Europe. He plays for Manchester United, Britain's most successful team of all time, along with such superstars as David Beckham and Ryan Giggs. Born and brought up in Tobago where he learned to play, Yorke was bought by Manchester for 12.5 million pounds. When interviewed about his successful adaptation to the limelight, playing for an internationally renowned soccer team, he said: "It's not pressure. Pressure is Kosovo, where people are not getting food and their country is getting bombed. I call this enjoyment. You play soccer, you express yourself in front of a lot of people, and you get paid a fantastic amount of money to do things you always dreamed of doing. That to me is a great time."

Less elitist are windsurfing and swimming, although swimming off the shore can be quite dangerous. There are windsurfing competitions in the islands each year.

Golf is also quite an expensive sport, and most people who play golf belong to an exclusive golf club. There are several golf courses in Trinidad and one in Tobago, all privately owned. There are no public golf courses.

Golfers playing the only golf course in Tobago.

SCOUTING

Most children in Trinidad and Tobago attend church, temple, or mosque, and a large part of their weekends are taken up with religious activities. Another activity for young people is scouting. The Scout Movement was introduced from the United Kingdom, where it was once very popular. The Scout Movement in Trinidad and Tobago has a strong following. Scout troops wear a special uniform, and their activities involve trips to the countryside, camping, and practicing Scouting skills such as flower identification, first aid, survival, swimming, and safety. Scout groups meet once a week in the evenings and study for a series of badges in each skill.

Scouting equips these children with essential skills for survival and teaches them independence.

QUEEN'S PARK SAVANNAH

Port-of-Spain is a dusty, busy city. Leisure activities are often centered on the Queen's Park Savannah. Some Port-of-Spain people say that the huge park is like an enormous traffic circle in the middle of the city and that all traffic weaves its way around it. The park has a circumference of 2.3 miles (3.7 km) and is the largest open space in the city. It was established as a park in 1814 and has served as the city's outdoor living room ever since. The park is useful for many leisure pursuits. During the hot working hours, the park is relatively empty, but after about 4 p.m., it comes alive with a myriad of activities. Part of the park is divided into soccer fields and they are constantly full of players. Other areas are dedicated to cricket. Joggers do circuits of the many paths around the park.

At the southern end of the park is the old race track. The races have moved to Arima, but the former grounds are home to all the biggest festivals in town and many smaller fetes. The streets outside the park are lined with vans and trucks selling plenty of good food.

Besides providing a place for leisure activities, the Queen's Park Savannah is also an excellent example of beautiful, classical Caribbean architecture, such as the building above.

FESTIVALS

TRINIDAD AND TOBAGO IS MADE FOR FESTIVALS both in its pleasant climate and in the disposition of its people. The really big festival in Trinidad is Carnival on the Monday and Tuesday before Lent begins. In total, there are 13 other official public holidays when all the workplaces close, shops have special sales, and special events and concerts are held to mark the event. Public holidays reflect the islands' cultural diversity with Muslim, Christian, Hindu, Catholic, and Baptist celebrations. A current issue is the lack of a special celebration for the Chinese citizens.

Celebrating a festival is not restricted to any one group or religion; festivals are celebrated by everybody. Indians enjoy Carnival as much as the next person, while Christians happily light a little oil lamp at the Indian festival of light, Diwali.

Left: Triniadadians participating in the lively parade of Carnival.

Opposite: A young band prepares to play at the Carnival celebration.

Above and opposite: **Carnival paraders, dressed in colorful costumes.**

CARNIVAL

This is really the festival to end all festivals. Trinidadians and Tobagonians sneer at the South American equivalents. Carnival has its origins in Europe in Roman times in the festival of Saturnalia, a midwinter festival celebrating the beginning of the new year. By the Middle Ages, it had become the Feast of Fools, a final celebration before the 40 days of fasting and denial of Lent. The event was always an outrageous affair, frowned on by the church.

French planters brought Carnival to Trinidad in the 18th century. Originally the festival was a serious religious affair with great balls where white planters wore fancy dress and impressed their neighbors. While the planters drank wine and wore masks, the slaves out in the yard had their own party which gradually took over the celebration in the years after emancipation. Over time African elements entered the torchlit Carnival processions which spilled into the streets with drumming, costumes, and lots of noise. Originally Carnival was three days of celebration before Ash Wednesday, but celebrations on the first day, Sunday, were banned by the British authorities. The more the authorities disapproved of Carnival, the more essential and wild it became, drawing in the descendants of the French planters and the middle-class colored population. In 1881 a group of British soldiers were ordered to calm down the procession but caused a riot instead. The authorities banned some of the more lewd characters in the Carnival procession, African drumming was banned, and finally the torches were outlawed as a fire hazard.

Carnival became a quieter affair but was never really quashed. In the 1890s a series of competitions was encouraged by the government to help clean up the event. First there was a band competition, then a calypso competition, then costumes, then others. In the 1940s someone discovered the use that could be made of old U.S. army oil drums, and the steel band was invented. In 1956, after a few war years when it was banned, Carnival came back with the Calypso King competition and has never looked back.

Every year, Carnival reflects the political issues of the times. In the black power years of the 1960s, the masqueraders dressed to tell the story of white control over the economy; in the 1970s they focused on women's rights.

HOSAY

When this festival was first celebrated in Trinidad in 1884, it was a sad and solemn affair commemorating the martyrdom of some early Muslim leaders. But after 150 years in Trinidad, the event has turned into a joyous and noisy occasion celebrated by all Trinidadians. In the past, wailing woman walked through the streets crying out behind replicas of the tombs of the martyrs. Nowadays fire eaters, Indian drummers, and whirling dances are the order of the day.

The festival begins with Flag Night when colorful flags are paraded around town to represent the battle of Kerbela. The next day a procession is held, led by elaborate models of the martyrs' tombs made from bamboo,

Trinidadians celebrating Hosay with a procession consisting of the elaborately decorated tomb and Indian drummers.

paper, and tinfoil. The procession includes dancers and drumming. On the third night of the festival, huge models of the tombs are paraded around the town, followed by two huge moons representing the martyrs themselves and carried by special dancers who dance around as if in a trance while carrying the enormously heavy poles with the moons at the top. At midnight, the two moons are brought into contact to symbolize the two martyr brothers' triumph over death. All this is done to the rhythm of the Indian tassa drums. Ghaka dancers perform a stick dance playing out a mock battle with stick and shield. On the final day, the moons and tombs are taken to the sea where they are cast on the water after prayers.

Corpus Christi, a religious holiday, is celebrated on May 29.

DIWALI

Between late October and early November, the Indian festival of lights is held to honor the goddess Lakshmi and to celebrate the triumph of good over evil. In the weeks before the event, Diwali Queens are chosen rather in the way of modern beauty pageants with the competitors wearing Indian dress rather than bathing suits. There are also concerts and musical competitions. On the night before, little oil lamps known as *deyas* are lit all over the house to light the goddess's way. All over towns that celebrate the event, the small lamps are supported by strings of colored electric lights. It is this show that has encouraged non-Hindus to enjoy the festival. On Diwali people exchange gifts, and there is feasting in every house.

Indians celebrate Diwali with a brightly lit replica of the goddess Lakshmi. Beautiful fan-shaped lights decorate the front of each Indian house.

EID AL-FITR

The festival of Eid al-Fitr marks the Muslim new year. Each year, the imams decide the day long in advance. The date varies from year to year, because it is determined by the lunar calendar. It is preceded by a month of fasting from dawn till dusk. On the day itself, there is a visit to the mosque, and alms are given to the poor. Everyone wears new clothes, and houses are thoroughly cleaned. There are official dinners at which people from other religions attend, and the traditional dish of *sawine* ("SAY-wine") is served. This is vermicelli boiled in milk with raisins, sugar, and chopped almonds. In private homes the family gathers for a similar celebration of the end of Ramadan and a sense of renewal and spiritual cleanliness. Unlike other celebrations, this one has not given way to the usual wild partying and remains a quiet family affair.

A mosque in Trinidad. After visiting the mosque in the morning of Eid al-Fitr, Muslim men return to their homes and join the rest of the family in a sumptuous lunch. Children are given candy and money.

FOOD

THE FOOD OF TRINIDAD AND TOBAGO REFLECTS the diversified culture of the islands, so no single dish represents the national cuisine. This is not due to any inadequacy in the food, but because many different cultures have influenced the kind of food that is eaten, the result is a mouth-watering blend of tastes and styles that includes African, Indian, South American, European, Chinese, and Caribbean.

The people of Trinidad and Tobago love food because it is a part of enjoying life and socializing with others. Any excuse is a reason for preparing something tasty to eat, and offering food to a guest is very much a part of the island etiquette.

Left: **A frozen treat being prepared by a street vendor.**

Opposite: **Hot sauces on sale at a roadside stall.**

CREOLE FOOD

The term Creole, when applied to food in Trinidad and Tobago, refers to those dishes and styles of cooking that have their origins in Africa. Along the way, European culture has also made itself felt, so that Creole cooking is an amalgam of different influences working on an African cuisine.

Pelau ("PEL-ow") is a typical and highly popular Creole dish that uses chicken, savory pigeon peas, and other vegetables along with garlic, peppers, and onions. The ingredients are cooked in coconut milk and served with rice. What gives *pelau* its appealing taste is the mixture of spices that are added. While the exact balance of spices is up to the cook, cinnamon is usually part of the mixture.

Cooking up tasty dishes in a restaurant in Tobago.

INDIAN FOOD

Indian food, alongside Creole cooking, is the mainstay of the national cuisine. While its origins and its vocabulary come from India, most of the dishes found in Trinidad and Tobago have a Caribbean taste that would not be instantly recognized by someone in India.

The *roti* ("ROH-tee") Indian bread, is to the islands what the hamburger is to Americans. It is found everywhere. *Roti* is affordable and is enjoyed at all times of the day or night. The *roti* is stretchable, and this makes it ideal for filling with curried meats, fish, and vegetables. There are different types of *roti*, but the most common kind is called *dhalpourri* ("dal-POUR-e") and is easily and quickly made using two layers of dough to form a thin sandwich of split peas. This tasty sandwiched bread is then stuffed with whatever ingredients the cook chooses. There is almost no limit to what can go into a *roti*; in addition to the usual curried beef, chicken, and shrimp, a more imaginative cook might throw in pieces of shark meat, pumpkin, or spinach.

DRINKS GALORE

The national alcoholic drink is rum, and Trinidad and Tobago produces well over four million gallons of it every year. Some of this is exported, although Trinidadian rum has not achieved the same degree of international recognition as that produced in Jamaica and Barbados. The usual lighthearted explanation for this is that so much of the rum is drunk by the people themselves that only a little is left for export.

Nonalcoholic drinks are not in short supply either. One popular thirst-quencher is made from the petals of the sorrel flower and another drink, called *mauby* ("MAO-by"), is an extract from the bark of the mauby tree. A favorite milk shake is peanut punch, and the sea provides another nutritional drink in the form of sea moss, which is liquidized and mixed with milk.

Trinidad and Tobago is blessed with a rich variety of edible fruits, and many are used to produce fruit juices. Mangos, guavas, and bananas are ubiquitous. Coconut juice is sold everywhere by mobile street vendors who use their machete to split open a coconut. Experience has taught them to recognize, by shaking the fruit, whether it is ripe for opening.

CALLALOO ("KAL-A-OO")

8 ounces (227 g) salt beef
1 tablespoon butter or margarine
8 ounces (227 g) okra
8 ounces (227 g) dasheen leaves (or spinach)
8 ounces (227 g) pumpkin
1 onion
2 cloves garlic
half a pint (237 ml) coconut milk
1 teaspoon sugar
tomato ketchup
salt and pepper to taste

Cut the beef into small, cube-shaped pieces. If you wish to remove some of the salt in the meat, you may first boil it gently in water for ten minutes.

Melt the butter or margarine in a saucepan. Then put all the ingredients into the saucepan and bring the mixture to boil before turning down the heat. Allow the mixture to simmer it for at least one hour. When the beef is cooked, remove the pieces of meat and blend the remaining mixture at the lowest speed on the blender. Return the meat to the blended mixture, and add salt and pepper according to taste. Reheat the dish before serving.

Trinidad and Tobago has a rich variety of animal life. Although hunting for food is not longer an essential activity, it remains a popular pastime because Trinidadians and Tobagonians like to cook and eat wild animals.

TRINIDAD AND TOBAGO

Tobago

Charlottevil
Speyside
L
Moriah
Roxborough
Plymouth
Buccoo
Scarborough
Canaan
Crown
Point

N

Caribbean Sea

VENEZUELA

Chupara Point

Matelot
Toco
Galera Point

Mount Aripo
(3,084 ft/940 m)

Northern R a n g e

St. Joseph St. Augustine
PORT-OF-SPAIN
Tunapuna
San Juan
Arouca
Arima
Valencia
Wildlife
Sanctuary
Matura Bay

Caroni Swamp
Caroni

Aripo Savannah

Northern Plain
Sangre Grande

ATLANTIC

Chaguanas
Upper Manzanilla

OCEAN

Mount Tamana
(1,009 ft/307 m)

Gulf of Paria

Couva
Couva
Central Range

Trinidad

Nariva Swamp
Cocos Bay

Navet

Pointe-à-Pierre
San Fernando
Princes Town
Rio Claro
Pierreville
Guatuaro Point

Ortoire
Mayaro Bay

Pitch Lake
Débé
Innis
Guayaguayare
Galeota Point

Point Fortin
Siparia
Trinity Hills
Trinity Hills
Wildlife
Sanctuary

Fullarton
San Francique
Southern Range
Moruga

Serpent's Mouth

VENEZUELA

Dragon's Mouth

Legend:
- Capital city
- Major town
- ▲ Mountain peak
- ★ Place of Interest

Feet | Meters
1,650 | 500
660 | 200
0 | 0

Scale 1:900,000

0 ... 10 ... 20 Miles
0 ... 10 ... 20 ... 30 Kilometers

Arima, B3
Aripo Savannah, C3
Arouca, B3
Atlantic Ocean, C3–D3

Buccoo, C1–D1

Canaan, C1–D1
Caribbean Sea, B1–C1
Caroni River, B3
Caroni Swamp, B3
Central Range, B3–C3
Chaguanas, B3
Charlotteville, D1
Chupara Point, B2
Cocos Bay, C3–C4
Couva River, B3
Couva, B3
Crown Point, C1

Débé, B4
Dragon's Mouth,
    A2–A3

Fullarton, A4

Galeota Point, C4

Galera Point, C2–C3
Guayaguayare, C4
Guatuaro Point, C4
Gulf of Paria, A3

Innis River, B4

Little Tobago, D1

Main Ridge, D1
Matelot, C2
Matura Bay, C3
Mayaro Bay, C4
Moriah, D1
Moruga, B4
Mount Aripo , B2
Mount Tamana, C3
Nariva Swamp, C3
Navet River, B4–C4
Northern Plain, B3–C3
Northern Range,B2–C2

Ortoire River, C4

Pierreville, C4
Pitch Lake, A4–B4
Plymouth, D1

Pointe-á-Pierre, B4
Point Fortin, A4
Port-of-Spain, B3
Princes Town, B4

Rio Claro, C4
Roxborough, D1

San Fernando, B4
San Francique, A4
San Juan, B3
Sangre Grande, C3
Scarborough, D1
Serpent's Mouth, A5
Siparia, B4

Southern Range, B4
Speyside, D1
St. Augustine, B3
St. Joseph, B3

Toco, C2
Trinity Hills Wildlife
    Sanctuary, C4
Trinity Hills, C4
Tunapuna, B3

Upper Manzanilla, C3

Valencia Wildlife
    Sanctuary, C3
Venezuela, A2–A3,
    A5–B5

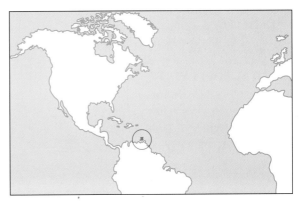

QUICK NOTES

OFFICIAL NAME
Republic of Trinidad and Tobago

NATIONAL FLAG
Red with a white-edged, black diagonal band from the upper hoist side.

TOTAL AREA
1,980 square miles (5,128 square km)

COASTLINE
225 miles (362 km)

CAPITAL
Port-of-Spain

MAJOR PORTS
Pointe-à-Pierre, Point Fortin, Point Lisas, Port of Spain, Scarborough

MOUNTAIN RANGES
Mount Aripo, Mount Tamana, Main Ridge

HIGHEST POINT
Aripo Mountain (3,084 feet/940 m)

CLIMATE
Tropical; rainy season (June to December)

TOTAL POPULATION
1,102,096 (1999 estimate)

INDEPENDENCE DAY
August 31, 1962

LANGUAGES
English (official language), Hindi, French, Spanish

RELIGIONS
Roman Catholicism, Hinduism, Christianity (predominantly Anglican), Islam

GOVERNMENT TYPE
Parliamentary democracy

POLITICAL LEADERS
President Arthur Napolean Raymond Robinson
Prime Minister Basdeo Panday

CURRENCY
Trinidad and Tobago dollar (TT$)
US$1=$6.24TT

MAIN INDUSTRIES
Petroleum, chemicals, tourism, food processing, cement, beverages, cotton textiles

AGRICULTURAL PRODUCTS
Cocoa, sugarcane, rice, citrus, coffee, vegetables

MAIN EXPORTS
Petroleum and petroleum products, chemicals, steel products, fertilizer, sugar, cocoa, coffee, citrus, flowers

MAIN IMPORTS
Machinery, food, transportation equipment, manufactured goods, live animals

GLOSSARY

callaloo ("KAL-a-oo")
A Creole dish made of salt beef, okra, and dasheen leaves.

dhalpourri ("dal-POUR-e")
A type of roti bread that is made using two layers of dough to form a thin sandwich.

Dih ("DEE")
A spirit believed in by those who practice black magic.

Diwali
A Hindi religious celebration, also called the festival of lights.

Douens ("DOO-ens")
According to those who practice black magic, these are the spirits of unbaptised children and they are malevolent.

Dougla
People of mixed Indian and African race.

Haile Selassie ("HIGH-lee se-LASS-ee")
The name of the former Emperor of Ethiopia, whom the Rastafarians believe to be God.

imam
A religious Islamic man who leads prayers in the mosque.

jihad ("JEE-had")
A Muslim holy war.

mauby ("MAO-by")
A nonalcoholic drink made from an extract of the mauby tree bark.

muezzin
A man who calls Muslims to prayer from the mosque minaret.

Mulattos
People of mixed race.

obeah ("OH-bee-a")
An African religious doctor who practices witchcraft and prescribes natural (herbal) medicine.

parang ("par-ANG")
Traditional Christmas music evolved from Spanish carols.

parranderos ("par-an-DARE-owes")
The musicians who perform Parang.

pelau ("PEL-ow")
A Creole dish of chicken, vegetables, and peas, spiced by pepper, garlic, and onions.

puja ("PU-ja")
A Hindu religious service that combines the worship of several deities at one time.

roti ("ROH-tee")
Fried, thin Indian pancake made from yeast and flour.

BIBLIOGRAPHY

National Geographic (magazine). *Trinidad and Tobago*. Washington D.C., United States: National Geographic, March 1994.

Saft, Elizabeth. *Insight Guide to Trinidad and Tobago*. London, United Kingdom: Insight Guide, 1992.

Taylor, Jeremy. *Trinidad and Tobago: An Introduction and Guide*. London, United Kingdom: Macmillan, 1989.

Warner, Keith. *The Trinidad Calypso*. London, United Kingdom: Heinemann, 1999.

INDEX

INDEX

INDEX